THE PREMISE AND THE PROMISE

Service of celebration at Symphony Hall in Boston, Massachusetts, May 23, 1960. Representatives from the Universalist Church of America and the American Unitarian Association gathered there to celebrate the consolidation of Universalists and Unitarians.

THE PREMISE
AND THE PROMISE

The Story of the Unitarian
Universalist Association

Warren R. Ross

SKINNER HOUSE BOOKS
Boston

Printed in Canada.

Cover design by Suzanne Morgan.
Flame photo by Diane R. Rose.
Other cover photos by Nancy Pierce/UUA
Text design by Terry Bain.

ISBN 1-55896-418-5

Ross, Warren R.
    The premise and the promise : the story of the Unitarian Universalist Association / Warren R. Ross.
    p. cm.
    Includes bibliographical references and index.
    ISBN 1-55896-418-5 (alk. paper)
    1. Unitarian Universalist Association—History. I. Title.
BX9831.R67 2001
289.1'32'09—dc21   2001020209

10 9 8 7 6 5 4 3 2 1
05 04 03 02 01

A different version of the chapter titled "Race Relations" appeared in the March/April 2000 issue of *UU World* magazine as "The UUA Meets Black Power: BAC vs. BAWA, 1967–1971."

Portions of "New Symbols, Words, and Songs" appeared previously in *UU World* magazine.

All epigraphs are from the UUA hymnal, *Singing the Living Tradition*.

To my fellow Unitarian Universalists, for sustaining a faith community that inspires us to cherish and strengthen the best within each one of us, and to work for a world in which the best in all people can flourish, and especially

... to Lucile, for fifty years of love, support, and joy, and to Catherine, Ellen, and Johanna for continuing to surprise me with the deep rewards of fatherhood ever since I first clutched their tiny bodies in my arms.

CONTENTS

FOREWORD ix

INTRODUCTION xiii

The Years of the Launch
THE PREMISE: A COMMON FAITH 3
SOME ASSEMBLY REQUIRED 13
A PIVOTAL ELECTION 29
A BITTER BATTLE ABOUT RACE 41
PAYING THE PRICE FOR FREEDOM 57
VEATCH TO THE RESCUE 71

Preserving the Future
NEW SYMBOLS, WORDS, AND SONGS 83
SHARING THE MESSAGE 105
THE LIVING TRADITION OF MINISTRY 123
WELCOMING THE NEXT GENERATION 137

Our Wider Horizons
THE EQUALITY CHALLENGE REVISITED 155
GLOBAL AND INTERFAITH CONNECTIONS 171
THE PROMISE: A FAITH FOR THE FUTURE 189

EPILOGUE 203

IMPORTANT DATES IN
UNITARIAN UNIVERSALIST HISTORY 207

BIBLIOGRAPHY 211

INDEX 221

FOREWORD

It took forty years for the children of Israel to make the journey from Egypt to the Promised Land. I'm not sure that the Unitarian Universalist Association is anywhere near the Promised Land yet. We do, however, now talk about the premise upon which the American Unitarian Association and the Universalist Church of America consolidated forces in 1961 and are working hard on "fulfilling the promise" of our liberal religious institutions.

What I identify with most in the old story, of course, is the fact that the leaders—Moses, Miriam, and Aaron—were not allowed to see the Promised Land. Perhaps none of us ever do. As Denny Davidoff and I complete our service as the most recent moderator and president of the Association, we know that.

We also know that it is important that we tell the story of our journey together—wanderings, murmurings, miracles, and all. After all, it is through mapping how far we have come and what mistakes we have made along the way that future leaders—and the people as a whole—can find direction.

At the age of forty, Unitarian Universalism is only now coming of age as a religious movement that is something new—more than the sum of the two faith traditions that joined forces to form it. It was born in the heady decade of the 1960s. It had moments— like the Selma Campaign of 1965—when its ability to forge interfaith cooperation for a more just and democratic society seemed promising. Unitarian Universalists often pass on the stories of our early history. We speak regularly about our roots in the Radical Reformation—especially now that we have such strong contemporary ties with the Unitarians of Eastern Europe. When Unitarian Universalists come on pilgrimage to Boston, it is often to touch base with our origins at the time of the American Revolution—and the mighty efforts to help make this a more democratic and inclusive society.

We are not so good about telling our more recent history. When I was helping finish a capital campaign in the mid-1990s, I found that one problem I faced was that many Unitarian Universalists did not know that history well enough to have a clear picture of the challenges and opportunities ahead. As we have begun to mature as a religious body and to think more strategically about our common future, discussing the past forty years of our experience as a movement is vital.

Because the events are recent, no one of us can or should attempt to render any final judgments, only trace some broad outlines and help us all to discern the patterns and possibilities. Warren Ross has brought to the writing of this account a unique combination of deep acquaintance with our institutions, journalistic skills, and the political acumen to know when simply to describe, and not to evaluate.

Forty years is a big, symbolic birthday for anyone. Though one hopes in organizations for a continuity bordering on immortality, forty years marks the time when many of our original founders are gone, and when the vision, the promise, has to be taken up by a new generation.

Our future leaders will need to make prudent choices about how to move us forward. May these pages, with their recording of how we have come to where we are now in the journey, serve to help us all realize the challenges they will face—and to commit ourselves to helping them, and all of us, to fulfill the great promise that still lies ahead.

John A. Buehrens
President, UUA, 1993–2001

INTRODUCTION

Unitarian Universalists may not believe, with Henry Ford, that history is bunk, but many probably do believe that history is for historians—not a matter that need concern the average member of a local congregation. We tend to ignore the warning of George Santayana that those who forget their history may be condemned to repeat it, or the admonition of Rebecca Parker (president of the Starr King School for the Ministry, our West Coast seminary), that there is a shallowness that comes from each generation defining itself, assuming it can ignore whatever came before. Putting it positively, Alice Walker said, "To acknowledge our ancestors means we are aware that we did not make ourselves."

Nonetheless, there may be an assumption that the history of an institution such as the Unitarian Universalist Association (UUA) is only for the specialist. The fact is that the forty years since the founding of the UUA have not only shaped the denomination we know today but have in large measure determined who, collectively, we are and what we believe. That is the story this book attempts to tell, a story that can inspire us with a renewed appreciation of just how rich a heritage we share. The values we derive from our Universalist tradition, historian David M. Robinson points out, include compassion, acceptance of others, and universal love, while we owe to our Unitarian forebears the emphasis on freedom of thought, intellectual rigor, and leadership in social reform. As Gordon McKeeman, looking back on close to sixty years of ministry and denominational leadership, has said, "We have a long and distinguished history and we need to articulate it for ourselves and for the world at large."

In any case, it's not just an institutional story but a story of fascinating, articulate people, people who shared dreams and visions, who faced crises and triumphs, and who fought out disagreements while still respecting the bonds of family—a faith family that embraces not only the UUA as an association but all our congregations and affiliated organizations. Fortunately, and that's what makes writing this history after forty years so opportune, many of them are still alive, preserving memories and anecdotes and at times vehement opinions.

The mainstay of this book is, therefore, a series of interviews, some sixty in all, with those who played a role in either the UUA's inception or its evolution. All direct quotations not otherwise documented are based on these interviews. Not only were the people interviewed tremendously helpful (help that is acknowledged on page 219), but these conversations turned out to be one of the real joys of working on this book. What a wonderful bunch of people have, in so many different ways, contributed to the success of the Unitarian Universalist Association! Warm-hearted, dedicated, proud of their contributions yet clear-eyed about things we might have done better, and above all generous in sharing their recollections and their time—I hope I have done them justice. I am particularly indebted to those who gave me access to their files. (A note regarding those interviewed: many are ministers and they are identified as "Revs." in the list of sources. However, so as not to break up the book with constant "revving up," we have skipped that nicety—in spite of protocol— in the body of the text.)

Many others also provided their help, but a few need to be singled out for special thanks: John Buehrens, who conceived of this project, supported it throughout its gestation, and made many helpful suggestions; John Hurley, UUA director of Information and Archivist, who was endlessly patient (and effective) in digging up books, documents, and all the other ingredients of the search for documentation; and Mary Benard, the editor at Skinner House Books, who found a way to suggest needed improvements while resisting the temptation to be a co-author. Thank you, John and John and Mary! Also, thanks to Maria D'Onofrio, who patiently and accurately transcribed all the interview tapes, and to Nanette Sawyer, who fulfilled her role as fact checker with both efficiency and tact. A word of appreciation is also due to the many UUA staff members who diligently answered my phone and e-mail queries.

And, finally, a disclaimer. History has been defined as a dialogue between an author and his or her sources, and no two people would have held this conversation in quite the same way. I came away with the conclusion that those who launched the Unitarian Universalist Association forty years ago did so on the premise that ours was to be a faith for the future. I also became convinced that if we live up to our potential, this promise holds true to this day. I hope that I have given enough of the context for my conclusions for all readers to hold dialogues of their own. Those who want to dig deeper should refer to the list of primary documents in the back of this book. I ask not for agreement, only for a renewed interest in our history. The more dialogues the better!

The Years of the Launch

THE PREMISE

A Common Faith

We would be one in building for tomorrow a nobler world than we have known today. We would be one in searching for that meaning which binds our hearts and points us on our way.

Samuel Anthony Wright, no. 318*

Even heretical and proudly rational religions have their patron saints.

Generations of Unitarians used to hang portraits of William Ellery Channing in their churches and fellowship halls, and many Unitarian Universalist congregations still do. Alongside Channing, you will often find a picture of the man considered to be the father of modern Universalism, Hosea Ballou.

And rightly so, for each formulated the essence of his faith not only for his own time, but defined the essential core that has remained relevant right to the present day. To cite just one example, it was Ballou who said, "If we agree in love, no disagreement can do us any harm. If we do not agree in love, no other agreement can do us any good."

* This quotation and all other chapter epigraphs are taken from *Singing the Living Tradition,* the current UUA hymnbook. The numbers refer to the hymnbook selections.

For much of the first half of the nineteenth century, as minister of the Second Universalist Society in Boston, as prolific author and editor of the *Universalist Magazine*, Ballou—untiringly preaching the good news of universal salvation—has been called by historian Ernest Cassara in his book on *Universalism in America* not only "by far the greatest thinker produced by the Universalist movement," but also "the greatest missionary that the liberal movement has produced." What's more, as Ballou's theology evolved, he also came to abandon the doctrine of the trinity, thus wedding Universalism to conceptual if not organizational Unitarianism.

Channing for his part preached the message of human dignity and the free mind, a unifying concept that gave the radical congregations of New England a positive common bond beyond mere rejection of the Trinity. It is a bond that is arguably still what holds our highly diverse denomination together, and Virgil Murdock in his 1975-1976 Minns lecture rightly called Channing's Baltimore Sermon "the most influential statement of the Unitarian position of all time." Moreover, Channing was one of the first to suggest that the liberal ministers of Boston form an organization. When a number of ministers and prominent laymen organized the American Unitarian Association, however, he declined to become its president—reflecting the ambivalence about institutions that has haunted the liberal religious movement ever since.

With both men occupying prominent Boston pulpits, it was no coincidence that they were well aware of each other. Ballou, for instance, published much of Channing's Baltimore Sermon in the *Universalist Magazine*, while Channing criticized Ballou's views of universal salvation as not conducive to the moral striving he favored. While they lived within easy walking distance of each other, it appears they never met either socially or professionally. Channing lived on fashionable Mt. Vernon Street, while Ballou's house was on a less distinguished side of Beacon Hill on Pinckney Street near the Charles River.

Therein lies a major key as to what kept the two denominations apart. As Ballou himself said, the social and educational differences between the two groups made most Universalists "little better than barbarians when compared with the graduates of Harvard College and other polished literati." That gap proved wider than the far more bridgeable theological differences, and still played a major role in the discussions that eventually led to the consolidation of the two denominations.

THE CREATION STORIES

Not only did each denomination have its patron saint, each also had its creation story. The Universalist account goes like this: John Murray leaves his native England in 1770 after the death of his wife and baby to start a new life in North America. When his ship runs aground off the New Jersey coast, he comes ashore looking for provisions and encounters Thomas Potter, who has built a chapel in the expectation that a preacher will come to testify to universal salvation. Murray is that man! Murray at first refuses, but when Potter persists, he agrees that he will preach on Sunday, provided the wind has not shifted enough by that time to set his ship afloat. It is a sign from God; Murray is still marooned and he not only expounds the Universalist faith he had adopted in England but is so inspired that he becomes an itinerant missionary, spreading his Universalist message from Pennsylvania to New Hampshire, eventually winding up in Boston.

A charming story—and we have Murray's own word that it is true. In any case, there is still a Murray Grove Unitarian Universalist conference center on the South Jersey shore to commemorate the event.

The Unitarian tradition, predictably, deals not with simple folk (the threat of debtor's prison helped drive Murray out of England) but with a king. Though Channing and other nineteenth-century Unitarians looked primarily to England for their religious roots, twentieth-century Unitarians learned to trace their origins back four centuries to the time of King John Sigismund of Transylvania. In a Europe torn apart by the religious wars following the Reformation, John Sigismund summons representatives of the major faiths to plead their respective cases for becoming the kingdom's religion. The Protestants and Catholics argue for their respective orthodoxies, but Francis David, speaking on behalf of the Unitarians, pleads for tolerance for all, saying, "We need not think alike to love alike." Persuaded that "no one shall be reviled for their religion by anyone," the king adopts Unitarianism and in 1568 issues an Act of Religious Tolerance and Freedom of Conscience, the first such document in recorded history. To this day, Transylvania is still a center of Unitarianism, with some eighty thousand adherents.

Neither creation story, of course, claims that there were no historic parallels or antecedents. John Murray himself records that when he reached Gloucester, Massachusetts, he found to his "great astonishment, there were a few persons . . . upon whom the light of the gospel [i.e., Universalism] had more than dawned." And unbeknownst to him, a physician, George De Benneville, had been preaching universal salvation in Pennsylvania since his arrival from Europe in 1741.

It was another immigrant from England, the renowned scientist Joseph Priestly, who gets the credit for starting the first congregations to bear the Unitarian name in North America. Fleeing mob violence in his native England—his home, his library, and his laboratory were all destroyed by rioters—he settled in Pennsylvania at Benjamin Franklin's suggestion in 1791 and started several Unitarian churches. Meanwhile, King's Chapel in Boston had shed all references to the Trinity or the divinity of Jesus from its Anglican prayer book and remains to this day on both Boston's actual and the Unitarian Universalists' metaphorical Freedom Trails.

Of course, what we wish to call the origin of Unitarianism depends on how far back we want to go. Before the Nicene Creed enforced the dogma of the Trinity, some early Christians —following the teachings of Origen and Arius—held both Unitarian and Universalist beliefs, and these persisted as heresies despite violent attempts to stamp them out. Even before that there were Judaic monotheism and a brief flirtation with the worship of a single god in ancient Egypt, but our true institutional forebears in North America are Ballou and Channing and their contemporaries.

CONFLICT AND CONVERGENCE

Universalism spread almost spontaneously as a response to the wide questioning of traditional authority, including religious authority, in the newly independent United States. Finding converts mostly in rural communities, it grew by 1888, Cassara reports, into the sixth-largest U.S. denomination. Unitarianism, meanwhile, inherited many of the organized parishes of the congregational "standing order" in Eastern Massachusetts as Calvinist doctrine became unacceptable to more and more of the Puritans' descendants. To this day the First Parish church on many a New England village green is Unitarian Universalist, while the minority that stuck to trinitarian orthodoxy had to go and found a second Congregational society.

Hence, for many years, Unitarianism remained focused on Boston, with Harvard as its intellectual center and its clergy mostly Harvard-trained, while Universalism flourished as primarily a grass-roots, rural phenomenon, the seeds being planted by itinerant preachers. Both groups lacked any denominational structure, but in 1825 a group of mostly Boston ministers decided to establish the American Unitarian Association for "the promotion of pure and undefiled religion by disseminating the knowledge of it." There was some debate about the new association's name. Some felt that *Unitarian* was derogatory, since it described a heresy and heresy in those days was still a serious matter. What's more, it was a name *intended* by opponents to be derogatory. The point of view that prevailed, however, was expressed by one minister who said, "We have, and we must have, the name Unitarian. It is not for us to shrink from it."

ONE HUNDRED YEARS OF COURTSHIP

Once one basic element of Christian dogma is called into question, it becomes almost inevitable that doubts are also raised about others. As already noted, Ballou joined the Unitarians in rejecting the Trinity, while the Unitarians shed concerns about eternal damnation in favor of moral striving in this life, often described as "right conduct." In addition, both groups made freedom of belief and conscience central to their religious convictions. When the Universalists adopted their 1803 "Winchester Confession," proclaiming that God would "finally restore the whole family of mankind to holiness and happiness," they added a "liberty clause" specifying that local congregations did not need to adopt the confession but could formulate their own statements of belief. For the Unitarians the principle that every congregation was independent and self-governing was retained from their Puritan founders' insistence on "congregational polity." It was a convergence of beliefs that led Thomas Starr King to make his often-quoted statement that "the one thinks God is too good to damn them forever, the other thinks they are too good to be damned forever." Himself the son of a Universalist minister, Starr King became minister of the First Unitarian Church of San Francisco, insisting on maintaining his loyalty to both traditions. He is widely credited with saving California for the Union during the Civil War and has been aptly memorialized in the name of the West Coast school for Unitarian Universalist ministry.

Inevitably, leaders in each of the two denominations saw the other as a natural ally. Thus began what was to become more than a century of flirtation—or perhaps minuet is a better metaphor, for it was a relationship marked by a continuing series of approaches and withdrawals, of asking first "why not?" followed by "why?" As early as 1856, fusion of Unitarians and Universalists was being advocated by some who pointed out that their theological differences were negligible. In 1878 came the first local merger, when the Unitarians and Universalists in Mukwonago, Wisconsin, decided to consolidate their churches. And in 1899, according to historian Conrad Wright, a resolution was introduced at the annual meeting of the American Unitarian Association, inviting the Universalist General Convention, as the national body was then called, to join in appointing a committee to "consider plans of closer cooperation." The following year, both denominations adopted resolutions stating that "closer cooperation is desirable and practicable."

It proved more desirable than practicable. A National Federation of Religious Liberals was formed in 1908 but died in the 1930s, followed in 1933—when both groups had been badly hurt by the depression—by an effort to organize the Free Church of America. Again nothing came of it, though in 1937 the two denominations cooperated in the publication of a new hymnal—the first time they had actually taken common action. In 1947, the two governing boards appointed a joint committee to explore union, but instead of union, in 1951 the national assemblies of both groups adopted a plan to set up the Council of Liberal Churches (CLC). Launched in 1953 at the first joint biennial conference of the two denominations, the CLC consolidated the departments of education, publications, and public relations. Like the Articles of Confederation that preceded the U.S. Constitution, it proved a halfway step that did little to add strength to either denomination, though hopes were high. As Alfred S. Cole, warning of the renewed strength and power of fundamentalism, pointed out, "If ever we needed to rally our scattered forces, our precious democratic traditions which seem to be going down in a savage reaction and fear, then that time is now." Stating the rationale more positively, President Frederick May Elliot of the American Unitarian Association (AUA) is quoted by Robinson as referring to the strands uniting the two denominations as "common memories and common practices—the things we do together as members of a free church."

In 1954, the two youth groups, having held their first joint national conference in 1951, showed the way to an actual consolidation, disbanding American Unitarian Youth and the Universalist Youth Fellowship to form a common organization called Liberal Religious Youth (LRY), while the combined college-age program was named the Channing Murray Foundation.

Finally, in 1956, the renamed Universalist Church of America and the American Unitarian Association agreed to establish a Joint Merger Commission—an acknowledgement by both parties that it was time to form a united denomination.

WHAT TOOK SO LONG?

Given their convergence of beliefs, it wasn't so much theological as socioeconomic and organizational factors that were the major stumbling blocks to achieving the desired union. As Ballou's bitter comment illustrates, the Universalists had long felt that the Unitarians looked down on them since Universalism, with a few notable exceptions, developed as a more rural than urban, more working-class than elite movement. Deeply dedicated to Murray's precedent of evangelism, the Universalists sent missionaries who formed congregations wherever their preaching could motivate enough people to join together. However, they did little to build any kind of structure, moving on to ever new localities and leaving their converts to fend for themselves. As a result, not many of the new congregations survived for long, and those that did were generally united by their passionate belief in a benign God and universe, but little inclined to institution building.

Nor did they have a pool of well-trained ministers to provide leadership. In fact, says Cassara, many Universalists were Baptist renegades, and "like the Baptists, many deliberately boasted of the uneducated condition of their clergy. In their view, the Holy Spirit operated freely among men and needed not the trappings of schools."

The Unitarians, on the other hand, having early on "captured" Harvard Divinity School, for many years remained committed to "the leadership of Jesus and the neighborhood of Boston"—a jocular takeoff on J.F. Clarke's once ubiquitous original, "The leadership of Jesus, salvation by character, and the progress of mankind onward and upward forever." The extent to which Unitarians represented the Boston establishment is illustrated by the fact that the UUA's 25 Beacon Street headquarters building is nestled between the Massachusetts statehouse and the official guesthouse of the mayor of Boston. When the statehouse was expanded in the 1920s and the original 25 Beacon Street was taken by eminent domain, the AUA was presented with a new site on the other side of the statehouse, the site of John Hancock's home. As a further sign of favor, the association was allowed to take along its original address.

Thus the two denominations differed in social status, in the role of the clergy, and in temperament. Emerson himself referred to "the icehouse of Unitarianism," and while he and his fellow Transcendentalists did much to warm it up, it still remained a self-consciously intellectual and elitist movement, proud of the academic credentials of its ministers and disdaining (with notable exceptions) the missionary zeal of their Universalist contemporaries. As James Freeman Clarke, then the secretary (essentially the head) of the AUA wrote in 1863, "The Unitarian churches in Boston see no reason for diffusing their faith. They treat it as a luxury to be kept for themselves, as they keep Boston Common."

When a union of the two denominations came to the top of the agenda, a widely held view among Unitarians was that Universalists were theologically too conservative, too emotional, and essentially "not like us." Many Universalists, understandably, feared that the more numerous and better organized Unitarians would swallow them up—"submerged not merged" was a popular phrase—and that as individuals they would be patronized. The widely divergent structural traditions were another problem. The Universalists were so reluctant to recognize any central organization that they had only recently changed their name from Universalist General Convention to Universalist Church of America. Despite the name change, their state conventions retained most of the money and much of the power. The loosely federated State Conventions were somewhat like a bunch of grapes, connected but clearly distinct, while the Unitarians were more like an artichoke, a cluster of separate leaves that at least gave the appearance of a single entity. Despite all of these problems, the logic of uniting finally overcame all biases and fears.

SOME ASSEMBLY REQUIRED

*As tranquil streams that meet and merge and flow as one
to meet the sea, our kindred hearts and minds unite to
build a church that shall be free.*

Marion Franklin Ham, no. 145

Question: If Winston Churchill had not replaced Neville Chamberlain as prime minister just before the fall of France in World War II, would Britain have held out against the Nazi juggernaut that dominated Europe? For that matter, if there hadn't been a Hitler, would there have been a second world war?

Similarly, if it had not been for two determined, self-confident presidents of the American Unitarian Association, would the two denominations have united? Leaving the debate about "the great man theory of history" to the historians, there is no indication in the record of any powerful grassroots demand to bring the two denominations together.

When Frederick May Eliot assumed the presidency of the UUA in 1937, the denomination had been badly hurt not only by the depression but by a loss of its sense of mission, even of identity. Having headed a Commission of Appraisal that called for a "Unitarian renaissance" and closer cooperation with other denominations, Eliot as president set about implementing the

13

Commission's recommendations. Believing strongly in merger with the Universalists, he called for "the uniting of our two denominations into 'The United Liberal Church of America.'" (Incidentally, Eliot's wife was a Universalist.) He urged, according to Robinson, that "if liberal religion is to play a real part in working out the destiny of democracy in America, it is imperative that our efforts be concentrated and not scattered."

Robinson points out that, by this time, each denomination recognized the rationale and possible benefits of consolidation, but each also understood the cost in unique identity that such a union might bring. "In the troubled 1930s and during the war," he says, "a simple survival was often a priority." Eliot succeeded in the establishment of the Council of Liberal Churches, but died soon thereafter. He was succeeded by Dana McLean Greeley, a member of the AUA Board and its secretary, minister of Boston's historic Arlington Street Church, president of the Unitarian Service Committee, and a proud fifth-generation Unitarian. A rising star in the denomination, he attended his first AUA annual meeting at the age of seventeen, became president of the youth group, and was only twenty-six when he was called to the Arlington Street pulpit to succeed Samuel Eliot, who had himself been AUA president and was the son of Harvard president Charles Eliot.

Greeley not only saw to the culmination of Frederick Eliot's vision, but as the first president of the Unitarian Universalist Association, put the stamp of his powerful personality on the new association. As he recalled in his memoirs, "I was to no inconsiderable extent responsible for the adoption of the merger plan," and while many others deserve to share in the credit, to a large extent he was right. It is worth, therefore, spending a moment to get to know Dana, as he was affectionately called by one and all.

To understand Dana Greeley it helps to understand the New England Unitarianism that shaped him. As Harriet Beecher Stowe wrote in 1826, "All the literary men of Massachusetts were Unitarian. All the trustees and professors of Harvard College were Unitarians. All the elite of wealth and fashion crowded Unitarian churches. The judges on the bench were Unitarians." While not as totally congruent with the Brahmin Establishment as Unitarianism had been in the previous century, there was in the 1950s still substantial overlap. At the time Greeley became its minister, twenty-three members of Arlington Street congregation were listed in *Who's Who*; Robert Bradford, senior warden of King's Chapel, was a former governor of Massachusetts; a state judge chaired the AUA board; a Saltonstall served as a president of the Unitarian Service Committee; and James R. Killian, president of MIT and science advisor to President Eisenhower, was the AUA's moderator.

Greeley acknowledged—and cheerfully accepted—that he had been called a nineteenth-century liberal, but above all, he was an optimist, capable of writing in 1971—post-Hiroshima, post-Holocaust—that "progress is the law of life." In fact, almost everyone who has written or reminisced about him describes him as "an incurable optimist." That's meant as a compliment, of course, and indeed it may well have been the trait that helped him to prevail in achieving the consolidation that had eluded everyone else for one hundred years. But think for a moment about the implications of that adjective "incurable." It suggests that optimism may at times have elements of the unhealthy.

Indeed, Greeley's optimism was not always healthy. So certain was he of the outcome of his policies that he seemed unable to comprehend why anyone would challenge him, even in the face of two crises that threatened to overwhelm the denomination during his term. Once he had decided on what he considered the right thing to do, there was no stopping him—whether it meant pushing for a union of the two denominations, giving shape to the new UUA with inspiring, even visionary leadership, or spending all its unrestricted endowment funds in hopes of raising ever more money. Of course, Greeley was not the only optimist and his fiscal policies were consistently supported by the UUA Board. One of his admirers (again thinking of it as a compliment) referred to him as "a man on a white horse." But we're getting ahead of ourselves. We need first to examine the horse, consolidation, before we can pay more attention to the rider.

A DECISIVE PLEBISCITE

While Eliot and Greeley may have been the major motivators, outstanding among the architects of the consolidation of the two denominations were Philip Giles, William Rice, and Raymond Hopkins. As general superintendent of the Universalist Church of America (UCA), Giles was Greeley's CEO counterpart. His, however, was a staff position by appointment of the UCA Board. The UCA president was merely the ceremonial head of the denomination. The relationship between the two positions is best illustrated by the fact that Giles's predecessor left the presidency to become general superintendent. As firmly committed to consolidation as Greeley, Giles told the delegates to the Universalist General Assembly at one point that if they passed up this opportunity to join forces with the Unitarians they might well die as a denomination. He was also one of the younger leaders who by this time had attempted to redefine Universalism as representing not just universal salvation but as a commitment to universal world religion. As Cassara describes it, the emphasis had shifted to a definition of Universalism "as boundless in scope, as broad as humanity, and as infinite as the universe."

William Rice was appointed head of the Joint Merger Commission in 1956. Raised as a Universalist, he was then minister of the Unitarian Church in Wellesley, Massachusetts. Under Rice's leadership, the Commission made two seminal decisions. The first was to enlist the help of professional consultants, and to get the two denominations—despite great initial resistance—to appropriate more than $50,000 to pay for their work. The second was not, as some opponents charged, to cast itself as a proponent of consolidation but to involve the local congregations in a wide and open dialogue, seeking all points of view. To facilitate the dialogue, the Commission distributed a stream of documents illuminating all aspects of the decision to be made. Then all member congregations were asked to participate in the decision by voting in two plebiscites. The first was to be purely advisory: Should the Commission proceed? The second was to be decisive.

The Commission's publications over a period of two years

included a 65-page report on the operations, finances, membership, etc. of the AUA and the UCA; an 85-page "Plan for Merger"; an 83-page summary of interviews with both proponents and opponents of the plan, together with an 11-page summary of the advantages and disadvantages; and a 139-page manual of background information for congregational study and debate, together with a 46-page study guide.

So thorough and persuasive was this preparation that 76 percent of the Unitarian and 74 percent of the Universalist societies participated in the first plebiscite, with 75 percent of those taking part from both denominations voting yes, the process should proceed.

Based on this approval, the Commission went on to produce a final 44-page "Plan to Consolidate"—widely known as the "Blue Book"—to be voted on by both denominations at separate but concurrent conferences in Syracuse, New York, in 1959.

Assuming the plan was approved by both sessions, it was then to be submitted to the second plebiscite, "in which each Church and Fellowship at a duly called legal meeting, votes approval or disapproval." The plan also included a proposed constitution and bylaws for the new denomination, with final action (assuming congregational approval) to be taken at concurrent business meetings of the AUA and the UCA in Boston in May 1960.

The proposed constitution provided that "the name of this organization shall be Unitarian Universalist Association" (since amended to the Unitarian Universalist Association of Congregations). This decision ended many months of debate as to whether to adopt a totally new name, such as United Liberal Church of America as Eliot had favored, to perhaps attract the Quakers and the Ethical Culture Societies. Once it was decided to keep the historic names so as to emphasize the historical continuity of the two traditions, the next question was which one should be named first, and whether the two names should be hyphenated. It was an issue that engendered much debate and high emotion, but the Commission's recommendation was endorsed both at the two concurrent Syracuse meetings and the subsequent plebiscite.

As a Commission of Appraisal report of 1975 concluded, "It is safe to say that there never has been a more carefully planned and thoroughly carried through process of decision making in the long history of the Universalist [and] Unitarian movements."

PLIGHTING THE TROTH

But we shouldn't pass over the Syracuse vote quite so lightly; the outcome was not such a sure thing.

A record number of some one thousand delegates—six hundred Unitarians and four hundred Universalists—gathered in a joint meeting to adopt rules of procedure and to listen to a report by Chairman Rice. They then split up first into small discussion groups and then into separate business sessions of the two denominations. Reporting to his Unitarian congregation in Knoxville, Tennessee, just two days after returning from the meeting, Robert N. West (later to become UUA president) described the session as "unbridled democracy in action . . . a Unitarian Council of Nicea, a parliamentary alley fight . . . and a heated family squabble. They were all there, amid the determination to produce a reasonably good plan."

Some fifty-seven amendments were offered to the plan as submitted by the Commission, and each had to be moved, seconded, debated, and voted on. And of course, since the Universalists and Unitarians were meeting in separate sessions, all wording, down to the last comma, had to be identical; any change made by one group had also to be adopted by the other. Only with such total agreement could the plan to consolidate— as amended, if necessary—be submitted to the second congregational plebiscite.

Among the more hotly debated decisions was whether to hold annual (the Unitarian model) rather than biennial (the Universalist model) General Assemblies. But only one issue almost caused deadlock, threatening to derail the entire consolidation process: the wording of the statement of Principles in the UUA bylaws. There were, essentially, three factions: the traditional theists, who wanted a reference not only to God but to our Christian heritage; the "universalist" theists, who preferred acknowledging the "great prophets and teachers of humanity in every age and tradition"; and the humanists, who would just as soon do without reference to any deity. So strong were the disagreements that the Merger Commission revised its proposal even before it was brought to the floor, then reverted to its original draft. That draft read, "To cherish and spread the universal truths taught by the great prophets and teachers of humanity in every age and tradition, immemorially summarized in their essence as love to God and love to man."

That made those who valued the Christian tradition unhappy for failing to pick up the phrase from the AUA bylaws, "which Jesus taught as love to God and love to man." They were even more appalled when the humanists and those fearful of a "creed" succeeded in passing an amendment to delete the paragraph altogether.

A highly respected group of more than twenty ministers led by Donald S. Harrington of the Community Church of New York moved an amendment to restore the original wording but to add to it a reference to "our Judeo-Christian tradition." They did so, they said in their petition, in order "to heal deep cleavages . . . which otherwise may seriously imperil the success of the merger effort and the general morale of liberal religion."

Harrington, though an enthusiastic supporter of consolidation, saw this as a point on which he could not compromise. Coming from a church known for successfully incorporating the wisdom of many faiths into its forms of worship, he recalls, "Our [Community Church] delegation was an interfaith delegation, as well as interracial, so this was not an issue we were likely to dodge." Not only a member of the AUA board, he was nationally known for such community activities as being president of the World Federalists and chair of the New York State Liberal Party, and thus his voice carried great weight.

Unlike the Unitarians, the Universalists had meanwhile blithely adopted the original wording by a margin of four to one and then sat waiting for their more contentious brethren to make up their minds.

Then, Harrington recalls, "We finally worked up wording acceptable to the Unitarian Christians and others as interested as I was in broadening the statement to indicate our openness and put more emphasis on the free spirit. When we had wording that seemed to satisfy everybody, I or some other member of our group moved to reconsider." That version read, "To cherish and spread the universal truths taught by the great prophets and teachers of humanity in every age and tradition, and immemorially summarized in our Judeo-Christian heritage as 'love to God and love to man.'" The motion to reconsider failed by seven votes.

Says Harrington, "By now it was very late and everybody was tired out." No wonder they were tired—the unscheduled session to debate this issue convened at 8:00 p.m. and was tied in knots until 1:30 the next morning. Though almost all the six hundred voting delegates were still faithfully in their seats, someone moved to adjourn. Raymond Hopkins, a key member of the Merger Commission and first president of the Council of Liberal Churches, spoke passionately against the motion. Had it passed, it would have been the end of the move to join forces yet again. Harrington remembers,

> I felt very discouraged and went to bed. About one o'clock, somebody pounded on my door. It was Percival Brundage [an AUA lay leader and former head of the Federal Bureau of the Budget] saying, 'Don, can't we do something about this?' and he showed me wording that he and some others had continued to work on. I said I agreed but that since we'd already lost the vote to reconsider I didn't know what could be done. At about three o'clock, there was another knock on my door. It was one of the leading Unitarian Christians and he said, 'Don, we've got better wording. Are you still with us?' And he explained that he had persuaded the Universalists to reconsider, which meant that the rules permitted the Unitarians to vote again, as well.

This version passed, with the critical passage reading that the UUA united "to cherish and spread the universal truths taught by the great prophets and teachers of humanity in every age and tradition, immemorially summarized in the Judeo-Christian heritage as love to God and love to man." Note that "*our* Judeo-

Christian heritage" had been changed by further amendment to "*the* Judeo-Christian heritage." It was a change that may not have made everybody happy but the plan to consolidate had been saved.

There used to be a joke that the reason Unitarians (which some now apply to Unitarian Universalists) were not too good at singing hymns was that they were too busy looking at the next verse to make sure it didn't need editing. Apparently the Universalists were less hung up on words and were willing to adopt whatever text it took to keep the Unitarians from blowing up the process. But Walter Donald Kring, minister of All Souls Unitarian Church in New York City, characterized the version he objected to as "anathemizing" Jesus. "To some of you," he explained, "statements of purpose may be simply a matter of semantics. To some of the rest of us, they are a matter of deep conviction." The problem was that others shared his deep sense of conviction but their convictions differed.

THERE NEVER WAS A MERGER

It was a noteworthy achievement of the Joint Merger Commission that it produced a plan not to merge but to *consolidate*. Raymond C. Hopkins, a Commission member and soon to become chair of the Coordinating Committee on Consolidation, explains why this change, apparently so trivial, was in truth essential.

A Universalist serving a consolidated Unitarian Universalist church in Brockton, Massachusetts, Hopkins had been chosen to represent the UCA on the Merger Commission. He recalls that previous attempts to unite the two denominations had been derailed by a legal problem. "Every time we got close to it, people in control would point out that you can't have merger. Frederick May Eliot, Dana Greeley, [and] Phil Giles all realized that if the two denominations merged, any two or three churches or intermediate organizations that refused to go along could go to court and say they were the true successors of the AUA or the UCA and claim all their respective assets." This was the reason, for instance, why Frederick May Eliot pushed for setting up the Council of

Liberal Churches instead of the merger he so strongly believed in—the lawyers had told him the AUA would lose all its money.

When Hopkins asked an attorney how the two Brockton congregations had managed to unite, he was told that they had not merged but had consolidated under a Massachusetts law that allowed two Massachusetts corporations with common purposes to do so, provided the state legislature approved. Consolidation would not legally terminate the two predecessor denominations and thus avoided the risk of a court challenge. Hopkins took this idea to the leadership and was told by the AUA legal counsel that there was no such law. But persistence and further research proved Hopkins right. As he says, "Without that idea of consolidation I don't think we would have got any further than any of the previous attempts." The change in terminology also pleased many Universalists who had feared that to be "merged" suggested being "submerged." Consolidation, they felt, had more of a ring of a marriage of equals.

Hopkins also explains why the opponents of consolidation— and there were many in both denominations—did not try harder in Syracuse to defeat the proposal. "They left thinking they had won!" he says. He explains that the Commission's plebiscite proposal required a 75-percent majority for approval of the plan. The opponents succeeded in adding a provision that 75 percent of all congregations had to vote, and as Hopkins points out that had never happened in the history of either denomination. In fact, the average participation in the annual parish poll was about 20 percent.

But they didn't count on Hopkins's skill and determination. As chair of the Plebiscite Committee he recruited two hundred ministers from both denominations and asked them each to be responsible for seeing to it that five congregations voted—not necessarily that they voted in favor, but merely that they voted. Then he found twenty area chairs whom he would call periodically to check on how the voting was going. The result, as he told Robert Sunley in his interview for David and Iska Cole's *Oral History of the Consolidation*, was that more than 90 percent of the churches and fellowships participated in the plebiscite. The proposal won by nine to one among Unitarians and eight to one among Universalists. What the rigorous voting requirements had in fact accomplished was to put beyond any doubt that consolidation was the will of the overwhelming majority of both Universalists and Unitarians.

The great emotional climax of the consolidation process came in Boston in 1960, when the two denominations voted to ratify the outcome of the plebiscite and to formally establish the Unitarian Universalist Association. Among the 887 accredited Unitarian delegates, the vote was 725 to 143 in favor. The Universalist vote in favor was equally overwhelming: 365 to 65.

What most of those in attendance remember most vividly is the worship service. William A. Donovan, later a UUA trustee and candidate for moderator and a fairly dry-eyed type, recalls the entry of hundreds of ministers as the delegates joined in singing the processional hymn:

> As tranquil streams that meet and merge
> And flow as one to seek the sea,
> Our kindred fellowships unite
> To build a church that shall be free.

"We sang it over and over and over again," Donovan told the interviewer for the Coles' *Oral History.* "There were people around us with tears in their eyes." Then he added, "I guess there were some tears in my eyes, too."

Preaching the sermon, which he called "Unitarian Universalism: Yesterday, Today and Tomorrow," Donald Harrington stressed that this milestone event was "partly a new birth, partly a commencement, partly a kind of marriage," but also "a degree of death, an end of things which have been precious to us." He then went on to speak of the new denomination's "tremendous potential, born of the world's response to our new relevance, caused in turn by this new world's need for a religion which is dynamic instead of static, unitive instead of divisive, universalistic instead of particularistic, history-making rather than history-bound."

After readings of "Voices of Our Heritage" that included Francis David, Joseph Priestley, John Murray, William Ellery Channing, Hosea Ballou, Theodore Parker, Ralph Waldo Emerson, and many others, the service ended with the delegates reciting in unison, "Let us together build the free and universal church of tomorrow. . . . We declare our allegiance to the new Unitarian Universalist Association, and pledge our lives, our fortunes and our faith to its high purposes and sure upbuilding."

COMPLETING THE STRUCTURE

Now that the Unitarian Universalist Association had been launched, it was time to make sure the craft was seaworthy and that the crew agreed on the course to be followed. Since the bylaws adopted in Syracuse only sketched the basic foundation for the new denomination, it was left to five interim committees to fill in the blanks. The committees were charged with making recommendations regarding nominating procedures, mode of organization, fundraising, regional organization, and ministry. Raymond Hopkins, undertaking his third major contribution to the consolidation process, chaired the Coordinating Committee on Consolidation, which pulled together the efforts of these five committees. The blueprint that emerged was presented at the organizing General Assembly in 1961, again in Boston. Philip Giles caught much of the exhilaration generated by consolidation when he called on the delegates "to unite in joy" for having crowned more than a century of cooperation and common goals with organic unity.

Like the Merger Commission, the Coordinating Committee sought to preserve the best elements of both denominational structures. They adopted from the Unitarians the idea of a moderator who would preside at meetings of the Board and the General Assembly (GA), and from the Universalists the tradition of a relatively weak president elected by the GA delegates, plus a chief executive officer to be named by the Board. Also, mindful of the criticism engendered by Frederick May Eliot's twenty-plus years in office and the way he (and later Dana Greeley) dominated the AUA, they set a proposed three-term limit for the presidency.

One person, however, strongly disagreed with this approach, and that person proved to be decisive: Greeley himself. He had every intention of becoming the first president of the new denomination, and he also had every intention of having all the powers he was used to exercising as president of the AUA. Not only was he both the ceremonial head and the CEO, he also served on the Finance Committee and took an active part in meetings of the Nominating Committee, as had Frederic Eliot before him, so that he could usually count on a relatively subservient board. The Universalists (and some Unitarians) thought that such concentration of power was not only excessive and dangerous but—in the words of one Universalist participant—"bizarre." But they were in the minority.

Even though Hopkins later served as Greeley's executive vice president and in many ways admired him, he still regrets that Greeley was able to insert three key words in the Commission's proposal—that the executive vice president would serve "under the President." However, Greeley failed to remove the term limit provision; in fact the bylaws as finally adopted set the limit at two four-year terms instead of the three originally proposed.

Another vital issue on which the Unitarian pattern prevailed was that the General Assembly would meet every year, unlike the biennial meetings of the UCA. An altogether new element was that GAs were to rotate around the country instead of always meeting in Boston as both assemblies had in the past.

Among other critical recommendations of the Coordinating Committee on Consolidation were these:

- *The Unitarian Register* and *The Universalist Leader* were to be replaced by a single monthly magazine.
- A Department of Service would take over the functions of the Universalist Service Committee, and the Unitarian Service Committee—which had been spun off as an independent organization—would be "encouraged to come within" this department.
- Roughly fifty districts would take the place of the Universalist State Conventions (a fairly autonomous group

with more money in many cases than the UCA) and the Unitarian Regions (also fairly autonomous, but with few exceptions without the independent means). These districts would be funded by the UUA but run by boards elected by the member congregations and staffed by a paid executive. There was some ambivalence as to whether these district executives would be answerable to their boards or to UUA headquarters or in some way both.

· In addition, there would be seven or so regional service centers directly administered by the central organization.

· As under the Unitarian pattern, a ministerial fellowship committee would extend fellowship to candidates considered qualified to have their names submitted to search committees. Under the Universalist system, ministers were "certified" by the state conventions.

Some of the other issues the interim committees needed to resolve were more technical but not therefore any simpler. To cite just one example, not only did the two denominations have different ministerial pension systems, but the Universalist pensions were administered by the state conventions. To make all these systems mesh without being unfair to anyone or diminishing their benefits was not an easy matter—and did not, despite great effort, leave everyone satisfied.

THE REMAINING CONFLICTS

What emerged, therefore, was a structure pretty much modeled after that of the American Unitarian Association, with some difficult final decisions left to the General Assembly to resolve. One such decision was whether, if funds for both were not available, the districts or the service centers would be initiated first. But by far the most contentious issue was whether the new denomination would have an internal service committee (following the pattern of the Universalist Service Committee) or one that was independent (like the Unitarian Service Committee).

To many it didn't make sense to have one such body as part of the UUA and the other competing with it. Moreover, the two organizations differed in philosophy, with the Universalists putting more emphasis on the use of lay volunteers, such as work camps for young people, while the Unitarians relied far more on professionals. The problem was that while the Merger Commission had opted for the Universalist pattern, Dana Greeley had promised the Unitarian Service Committee that it could remain independent, and therefore he fought the Commission's recommendation. There were those among the Universalists who considered this another symptom of "Unitarian arrogance," with some ministers going so far as to propose that there be a strictly Universalist organization even after consolidation. To assuage their concern, Giles wrote his colleagues that "consolidation *will* amount to absorption [but only] *if we allow it.*" While fending off the more aggressive Unitarians with one hand, Giles and other denominational leaders did their best to keep their restive troops in line with the other. For instance, Universalist minister Milton McGorrill of the First Universalist Church of Bangor, Maine, wrote his colleagues, "We ought to close ranks, pitch in, and do the best we can with what has come into being."

Another source of tension was that the UCA had recently gone through a wrenching but successful restructuring to put its budget in balance, while the AUA had habitually engaged in deficit financing—tension that was reflected in the exchange of memos between respective staff members. In one such memo, Mason McGinness, the AUA executive vice president, wrote to his Universalist counterpart, "We are not ready to give up a going concern just because the UCA program or experience . . . has been different." From the Universalist side there were complaints that AUA staff members seemed to proceed on the assumption that they would continue to operate exactly as they had before, consolidation or no.

Reminiscing about such critical and contentious issues, Giles, while expressing no regrets about his unqualified support of the union, does recall growing concern about the Universalist ministers being unprepared for the "hard-bitten internal politics that the AUA was not only used to but seemed to delight in." On the other hand, Giles concedes that the Universalist denomination did not have the dynamics of growth of the AUA, perhaps because "it was always bothered by its sense of failure."

Actually, the friction encountered in the critical months between Syracuse and the second Boston assembly was surprisingly mild, considering that it had taken one hundred years to reach this point. While there were, inevitably, instances of disagreement, expressions of fears and concern, as well as clashes of personalities, nothing except the debate about the wording of the Principles came even close to aborting the process. The final vindication was that only five congregations refused to go along with consolidation—and all but one came on board later. The founders of the new denomination had done their work well and by involving all the member societies in two rounds of plebiscites had assured that everyone could feel that this was, indeed, the sincere wish of both denominations.

The next step was to convene the first UUA General Assembly, which would make the critical decision as to who would head the new denomination. Another vital question—whether the existing regional organizations would turn over their funds to the UUA—was to be a matter of difficult negotiations.

A PIVOTAL ELECTION

Go out into the highways and by-ways. Give the people
something of your new vision.

John Murray, no. 704

What is striking is the extent to which the history of the UUA
mirrors the moods and events of society at large.

The early 1960s were marked by feelings of euphoria both in
our denomination and on the national scene. The nation's
upbeat mood was captured by the image of John Kennedy, our
young new president, going hatless in the snow and inviting
Robert Frost to read poetry at his inauguration. Dana Greeley,
about to become the first president of the Unitarian Universalist Association, inspired a parallel mood of confidence and
enthusiasm. It was a golden moment for both the USA and the
UUA; the tarnish came later.

Greeley's election took place at the first joint General Assembly in 1961. He was not unopposed, and the choice was bound
to have a profound effect—more even than bylaws and
resolutions—on the spirit and direction of the new enterprise.

Since there was not yet a UUA nominating committee, the
temporary bylaws adopted in Syracuse called for the appoint-

ment of a joint committee of eight, four members to be named by each denomination's board, to report its recommendations for nomination of the first moderator, president, and other officers back to the boards of the two associations. The two boards were then to "to determine by separate but concurring votes" the names of the candidates to be submitted to the GA delegates.

The Universalists felt strongly that if the head of either denomination ran for the presidency it might result in a damaging "us vs. them" confrontation, and Philip Giles, despite many pleas by his friends and supporters, refused to let his name be put forward. Dana Greeley, on the other hand, had no such compunctions. "I urged Dana to back out of it," Giles recalls, "because I thought neither of us should be president, that they ought to pick a third person, but he would never hear of it."

With Giles unwilling to run, the UCA Board nominated William (Bill) Rice. Widely respected as a superb chairman of the Merger Commission, he is described by Ray Hopkins in the Coles *Oral History* as "a hard worker . . . [who] had a presence and a voice that boomed." That much he had in common with Dana Greeley, but in terms of policies, he offered a clear choice. Unlike Greeley, Rice was committed to the weaker presidency envisioned by the Commission, while Greeley based his campaign on his vision of maintaining the growth momentum of the UUA. Rice also made an issue of Greeley's free-spending methods. Another item of contention was that the joint nominating subcommittee had split four to three for Greeley, with one of the Universalists and all of the Unitarians voting for him, yet Greeley consistently claimed to have been the unanimous choice. He was, however, the unanimous choice of the AUA Board.

When the votes of the delegates and the absentee ballots were counted, Greeley had won by 1,135 to 980. The UUA had opted for growth, charisma, and (the losers feared) control.

GREELEY TAKES CHARGE

William Schulz, later himself to become UUA president, tells a wonderfully revealing anecdote in his autobiographical reflections, *Finding Time*: "I once asked Dana if Debbie [his wife] had ever accompanied him on any of these grand travels, but before he could answer, Debbie spoke up. 'I went with him once to Worcester,' she said. Dana was slightly taken aback but recovered quickly. 'Don't be silly, Deb,' he shouted. 'I distinctly remember your coming one time to Albany.'"

Schulz also mentions that "Dana so loved the UUA presidency that he kept on his desk in Concord [where he assumed the ministry after leaving 25 Beacon Street] a clock stopped at the exact hour of the day at which he had retired from that office." Summing up his assessment of Greeley's larger-than-life personality, Schulz concludes, "What Dana did for Unitarian Universalism was to convince us that we were worthy of being taken seriously as a world-class faith."

In an even better position to assess Greeley's leadership was Ray Hopkins, who served as his executive vice president. The first thing Hopkins said when Greeley offered him the job was, "Dana, I didn't even vote for you." But Greeley held no rancor; anyway, he needed a Universalist to be number two in his administration. Nor was the election their final disagreement. For example, Greeley supported the initiative—adopted in 1968—to let the districts elect twenty of the twenty-seven members of the UUA Board of Trustees. Hopkins, on the other hand, was opposed to this reform, recalling that "I thought it would drastically change the nature of the UUA, making it a creature of the districts." But Greeley never held a grudge—and never changed his mind. As a result, says Hopkins, "Dana and I got along very well and had a very good working relationship running the denomination."

Hopkins's final judgment: "I've never met a man who was bigger, wider, more generous and more open than Dana Greeley. He had an ego, no question about that. But he never let his ego get in his way."

Philip Giles, Greeley's partner/contender in the consolidation process, who became vice president for Field Services in Dana's first administration—in charge of setting up the new district structure—also admired Greeley, with reservations. "I loved Dana very much," he reminisces. "He drove me crazy because I didn't approve of the way he operated, but he was a master at so much he did." By way of example he cites Greeley's prowess as a fundraiser and as an orator: "Whenever he left on a trip he always had a list of names in his pocket, and if the plane stopped anywhere along the way he'd get off and go to a phone and ask somebody in that community for money. And he could write a better speech on the back of an envelope than most people in a week's time." Giles also admits that he never, if he could help it, rode in a car that Dana was driving: "He used to scare the hell out of me. He had a great disregard for traffic rules; he was always too busy talking."

On a more substantive matter, Giles describes the way he and Greeley clashed on the question of the two service committees. Giles felt strongly that the Universalist structure should be maintained, combining the two organizations as a headquarters department. Greeley, however, felt bound by his promise to let the Unitarian Service Committee remain independent. Though he was a staff member, Giles asked Greeley whether he would object if he (Giles) argued for his position on the floor of the General Assembly in opposition to Greeley. Greeley was most gracious and didn't at all hold it against Giles that he publicly opposed him. But neither did he relent in his position, and he carried the vote. "By sheer will power," Giles sums up his reminiscences, "Dana got everything he wanted. Well, not quite everything, but just about." Such forcefulness enabled Dana Greeley to put the stamp of his personality and priorities not only on the UUA presidency but in many ways on the entire denomination.

MODERATING THE MODERATOR

But not everyone who disagreed with Greeley wound up loving him.

Marshall E. Dimock was elected as the UUA's first moderator. An expert on management, he had been a valuable member of the Interim Committee on Mode of Organization. As moderator, however, Dimock saw his role as a virtual co-president, demanding that he be given office space and staff. He interfered in the appointments of department heads, tried to get people fired, and actively opposed Greeley—whom he viscerally disliked—in board deliberations. After three years, frustrated by his inability to have his way, he resigned and disappeared from UUA affairs.

In a negative way, that confrontation helped to define the moderator's role. Dimock's successor was Joseph Fisher, economist and educator and three-term member of Congress. Fisher concentrated on presiding over meetings of the Board and General Assemblies, and in the contentious times that came later served a critical role as a universally respected conciliator and mediator. A trusted advisor to the UUA presidents he served with (first Greeley, then West), he saw no need to compete with them or promote his own agenda. He had quite enough to do—and to satisfy his ego—in his professional and public roles. For example, as chair of the Metropolitan Washington Council of Governments while de facto mayor of Arlington County, he was instrumental in getting the District of Columbia Metro built. In any case, he rightly perceived the role of moderator as that of the Association's primary volunteer, and not as that of staff member or co-president.

THE GREELEY AGENDA

As a primary policy goal, Greeley wanted to establish the UUA as a denomination to be reckoned with in the religious affairs of the nation and the world. The chapter headings in his autobiography, *25 Beacon Street,* reflect his priorities and include four that in a sense sum up his eight years as UUA president: "Race Relations," "Money Matters," "Peace Is Primary," and "Adventures in Ecumenicity."

His interest in interfaith relations went back to his years as a parish minister, when he served as president first of the Boston then the Massachusetts Council of Churches. As UUA president, he secured observer status for himself and other religious liberals at the Second Vatican Council, recalling that "I was sitting within thirty feet of Pope John as the Council first convened." He set up the Department of Overseas and Interfaith Relations, and traveled with Max Gaebler, its first head, and later Max Kapp, his successor, not only to Rome but to Asia.

The chapter on ecumenicity is studded with the names of important leaders he encountered and of significant events he attended. He says in his book that the high point was the banquet at the end of the 1965 General Assembly, and it was indeed an index to his success in reaching out to other faiths and being taken as an equal. Here is his description:

> Speakers included Bishop Frederic C. Lawrence of the Episcopal diocese, Robert Segal of the Jewish Community Council, and Professor Amiya Chakravarty, Hindu scholar and onetime secretary to Mahatma Gandhi. Dr. James R. Killian, our former moderator, former president of M.I.T., and scientific advisor to President Eisenhower, was a fourth speaker, and a fine one. And then it was my pleasure to introduce at some length Cardinal Cushing, who was the principal speaker of the evening. . . . At the conclusion we all joined hands and sang together "We Shall Overcome," and John Woodworth and his choir led us in a marvelous rendition of Julia Ward Howe's "Mine Eyes Have Seen the Glory." It was a memorable evening, denominationally and ecumenically.

Cushing's comments reflect the warm relationships Greeley was able to establish. Said the cardinal, "All of us have come a long way since the days of Michael Servetus, imprisoned and put to death by Christians, both Catholic and Protestant, for professing in his time that belief which is central to your concerns."

Summing up his desire not to be parochial, Greeley concludes, "My idol has been Channing, who said . . . 'I am a member of the Universal Church. No man can be excommunicated from it except by the death of goodness in his own breast.'"

PEACE IS PRIMARY

"I wondered at times," says Greeley in his chapter on peace, "whether to resign my denominational presidency to devote all my time to peace." He recalls Albert Schweitzer begging him when he visited Schweitzer's hospital at Lambarene in West Africa to "arouse the people out of their moral lethargy before it is too late." The looming threat that Schweitzer was referring to was, of course, the nuclear arms race of the 1960s, the time that school children were made to sit under their desks during disaster drills and Gov. Nelson Rockefeller of New York campaigned for a fallout shelter in every backyard.

But the term "peace" took on quite a different connotation with the outbreak of the Vietnam War, as it became the rallying cry of the burgeoning antiwar movement.

Calling Vietnam "America's greatest moral calamity," Greeley— a lifelong pacifist—began to devote much of his energy to supporting the protest against the growing United States involvement.

One galvanizing confrontation came on the campus of Kent State University in Ohio when National Guard troops fired on the demonstrating students, killing four of them. The student minister at the small Unitarian Universalist church in Kent was future UUA president William Schulz. In the wake of the shootings, the Kent city council banned all public meetings, but Schulz defied the ban by holding a memorial service. Like many of his fellow religionists and most of his fellow ministers, he felt compelled, openly and vociferously, to take a stand against the continued conduct of the war and the repressive measures of the government in response to the growing civil unrest.

President Greeley shared the commitment. Twice, at a time when such a move was considered by many to be nothing short of treason, he went with a team of religious leaders to Vietnam, though they were not admitted to the Communist North. He also took the lead in 1966 in forming the National Inter-Religious Conference on Peace, pleaded the cause of peace with both Secretary of State Dean Rusk and UN Secretary-General U Thant, and tried hard but unsuccessfully to get an interview with President Johnson. In fact, the chapter on peace is again studded with the names of famous (or then-famous) people, and with place names—ranging from Kyoto to Geneva to New Delhi—where he met with them. No wonder Ray Hopkins felt that Greeley left him fairly free to run the denomination. Adding his ecumenical and peace trips to his many domestic fundraising travels, he could not have spent much time in his office.

Greeley's right-hand helper in all these endeavors was Homer Jack, a UU minister whom he had appointed to head a new Department of Social Responsibility. A committed activist, Jack said, "It is not enough to write or preach about brotherhood and peace. One must try—however one can—to jump into the fray." And jump into the fray he did, in a lifetime of working for liberal causes. Jack's six-hundred-plus page autobiography, *Homer's Odyssey*, is an almost nonstop recital of demonstrations he led (including the first-ever restaurant sit-in the 1940s in Chicago), and of organizations he helped form (including CORE, the Congress for Racial Equality).

In 1960, after eleven years as minister of the Unitarian Church of Evanston, Illinois, Jack became executive director of SANE, the nuclear disarmament organization. One of the photographs illustrating his book shows him receiving one of the pens with which President Johnson had just signed one of the first arms control bills. When Jack joined the UUA staff in 1964, he remained equally committed to what the subtitle of his book calls his "quest for peace and justice."

DRAFT CARDS, SANCTUARY, AND CIVIL UNREST

While Greeley was working for peace at the highest level, a grass-roots anti-war movement was disturbing the peace in many UU congregations.

Arlington Street Church in Boston became a focus for this movement, certainly as far as the national media were concerned. Jack Mendelsohn, its minister at the time, recalls that the church was the scene of many anti-war demonstrations and rallies. "There would be a meeting going on in the sanctuary opposing United States involvement in the war," he recalls, "and there would be hordes of people outside opposing us and plastering the building with eggs. It required the Boston mounted police to maintain order."

The most dramatic event took place in October 1967. Students in the various universities around Boston who had formed an anti-war coalition received permission to hold a service at the church. Hundreds turned up who had academic deferments but who wanted to turn in their draft cards for delivery to the Department of Justice, so they would be held responsible for violating the law. One of them was Michael Ferber, a Unitarian Universalist youth leader who subsequently was tried and convicted, despite both Mendelsohn and Dana Greeley testifying on his behalf. (The conviction was later overturned on appeal.)

"The church was absolutely packed with students and TV camera teams," Mendelsohn recalls. "There were at least three hundred young men who took the solemn, perilous step of turning in their draft cards, but the media focused on the sixty or so who decided to burn their draft cards in the chancel, using a candlestick holder that was part of William Ellery Channing's heritage. That was shown on TV all over the country."

Mendelsohn opposed the burning of cards because he felt it was too theatrical, too self-indulgent. After all, unlike those who turned in their cards, those who burned them would never be known to the FBI, so it was not much of an act of civil disobedience. Dana Greeley, though sympathetic to the anti-war movement, turned down an invitation to participate in the service, feeling unwilling to support acts of civil disobedience.

Even more divisive was the sanctuary movement, which offered shelter to draft evaders and in some instances to AWOL servicemen. As the recently deceased Professor George H. Williams of Harvard Divinity School pointed out in a scholarly review, "The Ministry and the Draft," there was a long tradition of churches offering shelter to those being pursued, concluding that "the church can reconceive itself as a people of sanctuary for those young men of conscience . . . who sense that the present war is wrong." Arlington Street Church again led the way, but overall fewer than a dozen UU churches joined the movement. Richard Boeke, then the minister of the UU congregation in St. Petersburg, Florida, recalls that when his church offered sanctuary, it lost a number of its members—but gained a roughly equal number who joined specifically because of its courageous stand. At least no UU churches encountered the violence experienced by those of some other denominations.

Another source of conflict was that the Unitarian Universalist Service Committee (UUSC) had agreed to accept government funds for training social workers in Vietnam, which it considered humanitarian work, but which critics considered to be tacit support of United States policies. At one UUSC annual meeting a scuffle broke out when a protester carried a Vietcong flag to the platform. Later, opponents of federal funding, led by distinguished UU scholar James Luther Adams, staged a sit-in at UUSC headquarters. It was a rift that led to a serious loss of membership and contributions, and eventually the service committee ended its contract with the government.

Thus the conflict about the war led not just to disagreement but to serious disaffection within the denomination, especially among older, more conservative Unitarian Universalists, and it didn't make Greeley's fund-raising efforts any easier. As he ruefully remarks in his book, "I think [the Arlington Street Church] was never really conscious of how much the denomination suffered in its behalf."

MONEY MATTERS

Greeley may have regretted the impact of denominational dissension on fund-raising, but it did not lessen his efforts. He was, as Philip Giles has said, indefatigable, and Ray Hopkins adds that he in effect ran the fund-raising department. According to Hopkins, the Annual Fund went up by $100,000 or more every year while Greeley was president—but expenses went up by $125,000. The money was used to start new domestic programs and to fund Greeley's ambitious international efforts. He believed fervently in "investment spending"—building up the UUA's activities and funding the districts as rapidly as possible. Such a growth policy, he was convinced, would pay for itself in the end.

But it did leave a yearly deficit.

Some of the deficit was made up from the AUA's and UCA's unrestricted funds. Some more came from selling 16 Beacon Street, owned by AUA but used as the Universalist headquarters. A big chunk came from the Massachusetts Universalist Convention, the most affluent of the state conventions, though other state conventions, such as New York, were determined not to hand over their money. The Unitarian regions by and large had no money to hand over, with one exception: the Western Unitarian Conference. It not only had a large endowment but owned Lincoln Center, a famous settlement house in a black section of Chicago. A hotbed of Unitarian humanism at a time when the rest of the denomination was far more traditional, the conference had long fostered strong separatist sentiments among its leaders, and there had been a fierce debate between those for and against uniting with the Universalists, which the supporters of consolidation won only with difficulty.

Now the Western Conference was asked to turn over its money to the UUA. As Alan Deale, a retired minister and former UUA Board member, who had been instrumental in defeating the anti-consolidation forces, recalls it, "We decided we would cooperate with Greeley on the merger but that we would not give him our money. We had a feeling that Dana was a spender who spent very heavily and probably spent unwisely." Also, "We felt our money had come from Midwestern churches and we wanted the money spent in the Midwest, not piddled away on some pet project of Greeley's." To this day what is now the Midwest Unitarian Universalist Foundation holds on to these funds.

Another way the UUA supported its deficit financing and constant cash flow problems was through bank loans; Greeley with his Brahmin connections found them easy to obtain. While the UUA Board supported him, not everyone was happy with Greeley's brinkmanship. Ray Hopkins, as executive vice president, issued repeated warnings. "At the rate we were adding programs," he recalls, "I pointed out to the board—who didn't listen—and to everybody in the denomination—who also didn't listen—that the annual fund had to increase by at least $125,000 a year for us to stay even. Every time we fell below $125,000 would result in a deficit."

The problem, Hopkins feels, was that Greeley expected to have twelve years in office, but the bylaws set a two-term limit of eight: "He developed all these plans and then had only eight years to complete them. The last two years he was almost desperate, trying to accomplish all the goals he had set while time was running out. He increased programs faster and faster and he couldn't be convinced that it wasn't going to happen." Both Hopkins and Giles feel that if Greeley had had those extra four years he might have made it. However, Carl Scovel, ministerial colleague and son-in-law, doubts it. Indeed, he reflects, "I don't know if it would have killed him."

People have asked, both then and later, how the Board, the staff, the denomination at large, could have stood by so passively. Actually, the General Assembly did vote to add an elected financial advisor to the Board to keep an eye on things, but by that time it was too late. Giles, in retrospect, reflects that "Dana's staff was as puzzled by him as others were. He was a man of enormous charisma, even among those of us who disagreed with him on various gambits that he took. Some of us tried to dissuade him from some of those tacks—vigorously at times, with heat at times. He never held it against us, but by the same token, he never gave an inch."

Hopkins makes an additional point: "Everybody blames Dana [for the inevitable financial crisis soon to come]. But the Board supported all these things. The General Assembly supported all these things. He was so convincing."

The one issue on which Greeley could not persuade his critics was the racial crisis that shook the UUA toward the end of his second term, causing a rift that threatened the denomination's very existence.

A BITTER BATTLE ABOUT RACE

Those who profess to favor freedom, and yet deprecate
agitation, are people who want crops without plowing up
the ground.

Frederick Douglass, no. 579

Once again the denomination's experience reflected that of the country at large. When people who have joined the Unitarian Universalist movement since 1969 hear that there was a major walkout at General Assembly they find it hard to believe. What? Among Unitarian Universalists? People seized microphones? Called each other unforgivable names? Spat in each other's face? How could that be?

Perhaps a brief recital of the national events that formed the background for our troubles will make it more comprehensible: 1969 was the year of the Woodstock Festival, where unexpectedly some five hundred thousand "kids" showed up to take off their clothes, smoke pot, and revel in the mud to the beat of rock and roll. It was the year of the police raid on the Stonewall Inn, a gay bar in New York's Greenwich Village, triggering the gay pride movement; the year of the largest ever anti-Vietnam war demonstration in Washington, D.C.; and the year of the trial of the antiwar demonstrators who had battled the police at the Chicago

Democratic convention the year before. In the 1968 presidential election following that convention, Richard Nixon and George Wallace between them won almost 60 percent of the vote.

It was a year, in other words, when turmoil and contention were endemic and when slogans such as "if you're not part of the solution you are part of the problem" seemed to require anyone with a conscience not only to speak out but, for those who felt most strongly, to act up. Meanwhile the national commitment in favor of civil rights was turning into angry confrontation. Whereas the struggle for racial justice and equal rights in the South had united the UU denomination and sustained its self-image of "us" (the good guys) vs. "them" (the racists), the black power movement's demands for black empowerment split Unitarian Universalists, both white and black, who almost overnight were fighting among themselves, calling each other racist and fascist and inflicting wounds that have still not entirely healed.

Two tragic events mark the arc of this turnabout. First, in 1965, came the murder of UU minister James Reeb while he was in Selma, Alabama, demonstrating for black voting rights. The second occurred only four years later when many black delegates and their white supporters walked out of the General Assembly in Boston to protest what they considered to be a racist vote. It is a painful story but no history of the UUA is complete without it.

Universalists and Unitarians had, of course, become involved in the fight for racial justice long before 1965. Back in the mid-nineteenth century, ministers of both denominations adopted antislavery declarations, and in 1963, busloads of Unitarian Universalists descended on Washington, D.C., to join in the biggest civil rights demonstration in the nation's history and to hear Martin Luther King deliver his "I Have a Dream" oration. But the climax came two years later, when black demonstrators were stopped by police using clubs and tear gas as they tried to march from Selma to Montgomery, Alabama, to petition for voting rights. King sent a telegram to religious leaders asking for support. "In the vicious maltreatment of defenseless citizens of Selma, where old women and young children were gassed and clubbed at random," he said, ". . . it is fitting that all Americans help to bear the burden." Homer Jack, having just recently joined the UUA staff, immediately urged UU ministers to join him in Alabama. "The Monday evening when we arrived in Selma's Brown Chapel, among the first whites to do so," he recalls in his autobiography, "we were greeted eagerly, warmly, by the over-flowing church full of Negroes, some of whom were brutalized by state police only the day before."

Roughly 100 UU ministers heeded King's call, including Orloff Miller, Clark Olsen, and James Reeb. They were joined by some 100 lay Unitarian Universalists and 350 clergy and religious from other denominations. Here is Miller's recollection of the events of March 9, 1965:

> As Clark, Jim, and I left Walker's Café we were attacked by four or five segregationist bigots. Jim's skull was crushed with the blow of a club from behind. Clark and I, having escaped with only scrapes and bruises, managed to get help for Jim—but he died two days later at Alabama's University Hospital in Birmingham.
>
> Jim's death galvanized the nation—a nation which had hardly noticed a few days before when Jimmy Lee Jackson, a local Negro, had been shot and killed during a similar demonstration—but James Reeb was a white minister from the North, and President Johnson sent yellow roses to his hospital room.

Viola Gregg Liuzzo, a Unitarian Universalist from Detroit, was also killed. Submitting new voting rights legislation to Congress, President Johnson declared the events in Selma "an American tragedy" which should strengthen people's determination "to bring full and equal and exact justice to all of our people."

By coincidence, the UUA Board was meeting in Boston the day after Reeb's death, and the members, deciding that they, too, had to bear witness, adjourned to Selma. Here is how Dana Greeley remembered what happened when they got there: "The next day . . . a procession was formed—I suppose at least a thousand people. I was in the front line . . . and marched to the Selma Wall, the police barricade beyond which the police would not let us pass. There we had a real confrontation. We were met by state troopers, with all their weapons," who refused to let them pass. At the memorial service for Reeb two days later, "Martin Luther King gave the stirring memorial address. It was my assignment to give the main prayer. There has not been in recent Unitarian Universalist civil rights history another incident like the Reeb martyrdom," Greeley goes on in his memoirs, "but I do believe that many ministers have been as dedicated as James Reeb was and that our laymen [sic] and our churches and fellowships through many years contributed proportionately at least as much as any denomination to progress in this area."

Thus the martyrdom of Reeb became enshrined as proof of our "racial sanctity," along with the famous story of how Theodore Parker wrote his sermons with a pistol in his desk drawer to fight off anyone trying to recapture the fugitive slaves he was harboring. Parker, renowned as the most charismatic Unitarian preacher of the mid-nineteenth century, said of his colleague Ezra Stiles Gannett, "Yes, he is calling on his church members to kidnap mine." What we recall less often is that Gannett, too, was Unitarian, as was George Ticknor, slave commissioner for Boston. Gannett, by the way, foreshadowing the pain of many Unitarian Universalists as they struggled with conflicting impulses one hundred years later, agonized over his position that preservation of the Union must take precedence over the freedom of fugitives. In a letter to his daughter he said that if a fugitive came to his door, "I should shelter him and aid him to go further on to Canada, and then I should go and give myself up to prison."

It did not take long before Unitarian Universalists of the 1960s were made aware that they, too, faced a moral dilemma. The comfortable assumption that they were on the right side of the civil rights struggle was badly shaken by statements like that of Heyward Henry, chair of the newly formed Black Unitarian Universalist Caucus in 1968. Said Henry, "We Unitarian Universalists like to keep saying, 'But we went to Selma with you . . . why are you [blacks] rejecting us?' In Selma, a black man named Jimmy Jackson was killed and at that time you could count the number of Unitarians in Selma on your fingers. A few weeks later

a white man was killed and all Unitarians ran to Selma. Racism,
that's what it was."

FROM SELMA TO THE BILTMORE

Another challenge came from those who pointed out that while
we were indeed well represented in the struggle for civil rights,
our congregations remained overwhelmingly white, and that
only a handful of African Americans had ever been ordained as
either Unitarian, Universalist, or Unitarian Universalist ministers. In any case, accusations such as those of Heyward Henry
were met not only by white Unitarian Universalists but also by
many black members with anger and disbelief, but mostly—
"Who? Us?"—consternation.

Part of the problem may also have been that the progression
from the civil rights agenda to calls for black empowerment was
so swift. Even as Martin Luther King led the civil rights march in
Washington, Malcolm X was preaching not integration but separatism, Black Panther violence made headlines, and racial riot-
ing left twenty-three dead in Newark, forty-three dead in Detroit.
Two years later, the murder of James Meredith enraged black
Americans, and King in the months before his assassination was
being pushed by younger supporters to abandon his tactics of
nonviolence and alliances with whites. Starting in Los Angeles,
some black Unitarian Universalists echoed this impatience. As
Mark Morrison-Reed points out in his book *Black Pioneers in a
White Denomination,* "We do not stand above the social attitudes
of our times, as we are prone to believe, but instead flounder
about in their midst with everyone else."

And flounder we did. In response to the turmoil, the Unitarian Universalist Commission on Religion and Race called an
Emergency Conference on Unitarian Universalist Response to
the Black Rebellion. In October of 1967, some 135 participants
including thirty-seven African Americans gathered at New York's
Biltmore Hotel. District executives had picked seventy-six of
them; twenty-six were UUA staff or committee members; the rest
were ecumenical observers or black theological students.

Whether or not they fairly represented the denomination was hotly debated and is still a matter of contention.

Homer Jack was director of the conference; presiding over it was Cornelius McDougald, chair of the Commission on Religion and Race and board chair of the Community Church in New York City. Almost immediately, however, at the call of black people from Los Angeles, thirty of the thirty-seven African American delegates withdrew to form a caucus closed to whites. There they developed a list of what they called "non-negotiable demands" that they announced would have to be accepted or rejected by the conference in toto for submission to the UUA Board of Trustees. The core demand was that the Board establish a Black Affairs Council (BAC), to be appointed by the Black Unitarian Universalist Caucus (BUUC), and to be funded for four years at $250,000 a year. When the delegates who had not left the conference in protest finally reconvened, these demands were adopted. As Victor Carpenter, now the senior minister in Belmont, Massachusetts, was to say in his Minns lecture of 1983, "The conference itself had been called to confront a general problem, namely the racial dilemma confronting the country. To this general issue the [black] middle-class Unitarian Universalists . . . brought a specific agenda—their personal quest for self-discovery as black Unitarian Universalists." And Henry Hampton, then the UUA's director of information and also a Black Caucus supporter, said, "Black people at the conference became full-fledged liberals, for the first time [able] to determine their course."

McDougald, also an African American, was among those who refused to join the caucus, saying he was unwilling "to submit to intimidation by blacks or whites." Thus began a split among black Unitarian Universalists that soon threatened to tear the entire denomination apart. It's a split well illustrated by the different reactions of two black delegates from the Community Church, which had a membership that was twenty-five percent black and prided itself on its effectiveness as a force for racial justice. (Its previous minister, John Haynes Holmes, was a co-founder of the NAACP.) Maude Jenkins, a retired physician, recalls being so upset by the caucus tactics that "it took me months to recuperate." Winifred Latimer Norman, on the other hand—never having seen more than a handful of other black people at General Assemblies—was so thrilled by seeing so many of them at a UU function that it "definitely persuaded me to support" the quest for black empowerment. And so Norman, who later served on the UUA Board, became a leader in the Black Affairs Council, while McDougald became co-chair of what was at first called Black and White Alternative, then Black and White Action. Those conflicting initials—BAC and BAWA—for some ten years signified the most heated and irreconcilable division in the denomination's history.

In an attempt to dampen the flames ignited at the Biltmore, Homer Jack circulated a response in which he first listed the most common criticisms of the Black Caucus: that it was not merely separatist but racist, that it was totalitarian in its methods, and that it spoke for only a fraction of black Unitarian Universalists. To which he offered these rejoinders: that separatism was a tactic, not a goal; that there was precedent "for cabals, secret caucuses—and worse" within our denomination; and that thirty out of the thirty-seven black people at the Emergency Conference had joined the Caucus. Jack also pointed out that "revolutions are never reasonable or rational," but appeals for forbearance came too late. A 1983 Commission on Appraisal report published by the UUA together with Carpenter's lecture as *Unitarian Universalism and the Quest for Racial Justice* concluded, "Sides had been chosen and alternatives were not to be explored. Confrontation [was] . . . in the air."

A CHRONOLOGY

Since the wounds of this split have not yet wholly healed, it is probably impossible to describe the events to everyone's satisfaction, but at least we can construct a simple recital of the recorded facts, leaning heavily on the report of the Commission of Appraisal and Carpenter's lectures.

1967: The UUA Board responds to the Biltmore Conference report by voting to reorganize the Commission on Religion and Race by adding "substantial participation of non-whites," but not to form a Black Affairs Council and refusing the request for a million dollars. But the Board is not unanimous. While vice moderator Wade McCree, its only black member and a U.S. Circuit Court judge, later to become solicitor general of the United States, threatens to resign if the Caucus demands are met, trustee Carleton Fisher says that if it were *not* done it would "rather conclusively indicate that we have lost touch completely with the very ground of our faith as Unitarian Universalists." Adding to the tension, the Black Unitarian Universalist Caucus then urges its supporters to boycott the UUA Annual Fund.

The same year, a group of white people endorses the BUUC agenda, launching FULLBAC ("Full Support of BAC"). This, too, proves controversial. For instance, Betty Bobo Seiden, a black BAWA leader, writes, "You say that we blacks are supposed to be off getting ourselves equal to you. I feel equal right now. . . . Can you see how insulted I am that your Lady Bountiful basket is going to give me self-empowerment?"

1968: Passions run high at the General Assembly in Cleveland, "the year of ministerial turtleneck shirts and of buttons," in the words of Homer Jack. Everyone on both sides of the issue realizes that this is a watershed event in the life of the denomination. Despite efforts by the Board and President Greeley to substitute voluntary fund-raising for the caucus proposal and to accept both BAC and BAWA as affiliate members, the delegates vote 836 to 326 to form a Black Affairs Council to be funded at $250,000 a year for four years, while BAWA is to get nothing.

1969: The official agenda at the General Assembly in Boston calls for the appropriation of another quarter million for BAC and $50,000 for BAWA, but BAC insists that it will not accept funding if BAWA is to get even a penny. As soon as the business session is called to order, there's a motion from the floor to put this item first on the agenda. When the motion fails, a substantial number of delegates walk out, though they return later. At another point, BAC chair Heyward Henry announces that "the microphones will be possessed," and members of BUUC and of Liberal Religious Youth, the UU young people's group, stand at each of the floor mikes to prevent anyone else from speaking. When the black co-chair of BAWA insists on being heard, the BUUC/FULLBAC delegates again walk out. Eventually, the vote to fund BAC but not BAWA passes. On the other hand, in an apparent contradiction, the delegates elect Robert West as UUA president, defeating Aron Gilmartin, the pro-BUUC/FULLBAC candidate (as well as five others), even though West's platform calls for securing future BAC funding not from the UUA budget but through voluntary campaigns.

1969: Faced with a substantial deficit and the depletion of unrestricted funds, the UUA Board votes in November—as part of cuts representing one-third of the budget—to reduce the BAC allocation by $50,000 and to meet the million-dollar obligation in five years rather than four. Henry calls this a "shocking revelation of the institutional racism still rampant in the UUA," and BAC moves to disaffiliate.

1970: Meeting in Seattle, Washington, the General Assembly rejects a motion to restore full funding to the Black Affairs Council.

1971: With the issue again on the GA agenda, the delegates adopt a resolution to set up a Fund for Racial Justice "to finance all Unitarian Universalist efforts . . . to achieve racial justice," to be conducted in partnership with both BAC and BAWA. The UU Society at Shelter Rock, New York (then called the North Shore Society), contributes $250,000 to this fund and the UUA Board votes to give $180,000 to BAC and $45,000 to BAWA. BAC sends out a press release saying, "Our religious movement has experienced serious schism around this issue, and the North Shore Unitarian

Church action will do much by way of healing some of the wounds."

1968-72: Controversy breaks out about BAC's accounting for the money it has received. BAC's critics demand better reporting, while its defenders claim that no other UUA affiliate organization has been asked for audits. The Commission on Appraisal eventually publishes a recap of BAC income and expenses for 1968 to 1972, but since it includes such catch-all items as "nineteen grants—$137,147.99," it doesn't resolve the controversy. (One BAC grant supports the California academician who develops the concept of Kwanzaa; another goes to Henry Hampton, former UUA director of communications, who later produced "Eyes on the Prize," the highly praised series of public television documentaries on the civil rights struggle.)

1971-1979: A split develops in the BAC leadership, leading to the setting up of a rival organization, followed by lawsuits over control of funds and charges of misappropriation. Both BAC and FULLBAC cease to function, but BAWA remains active for several more years, producing anti-racist TV public service announcements and, at the 1977 General Assembly, sponsoring a lecture by Arthur S. Fleming, chair of the U.S. Civil Rights Commission. In 1979 BAWA sponsors a twenty-fifth anniversary celebration in Topeka, Kansas, of the Supreme Court's Brown vs. Topeka Board of Education school desegregation decision. It was, Max Gaebler—one of the organization's leaders—recalls, "BAWA's swan song."

THE FACTS THROUGH DIFFERENT LENSES

Those, highly condensed, are some key facts, and facts supposedly don't lie. But they don't tell the entire truth either. To grasp the pain and fury that were felt we need to go to the recollections of some of the participants in these events. Here is how President Greeley describes the walkout at the Boston General Assembly in his autobiography:

There were two most shocking moments for me in the Assembly. One occurred when a young black delegate took one of the floor microphones forcibly, put it under his coat, and wouldn't release it. I had not expected ever to see that kind of act at one of our meetings. . . . The second shock came during a speech of Jack Mendelsohn's from the rostrum . . . [who] indicated that he was discouraged and was going to leave the Assembly, boycott it, and anybody who wanted to leave with him was welcome to do so. . . . Here was my minister, walking out on my administration and my Board and my Assembly (and his), and going over to my [Arlington Street] church (and his) for a rump session or to form a dissident or splinter group.

Greeley and moderator Joseph Fisher later led a delegation that went to Arlington Street Church and persuaded the dissidents to return the next day. Fisher, while not neutral, was widely respected for his fairness and patience as presiding officer, but his calm was only outward. As his widow, Margaret Fisher, recalls in a letter to John Buehrens, "Joe agonized over the demands and the walkouts. He and Dana pled and wept as their efforts at reconciliation were turned to humiliation." The stress was hard to bear. "I intercepted phone calls at 4:00 a.m.," Margaret Fisher goes on, "demanding that Joe go right then and there to the Arlington Street Church where the BAC/BUUC leaders were holding out. I refused to awaken him, stating that he could not preside over three thousand delegates without a night's sleep."

Fisher's role in holding the denomination together was so widely acknowledged that when his term ended the UUA Nominating Committee pleaded with him to let himself be renominated, and despite all his other obligations he reluctantly agreed.

Jack Mendelsohn, Greeley's successor as minister of the Arlington Street Church and co-chair of Greeley's presidential campaign, had by now become vice chair of the Black Affairs Council. His recollections agree with Greeley's on very little except the high pitch of the emotions. Insisting that he knew of no prior plans for a walkout he recalls,

Almost all of the two hundred to three hundred black delegates who were there got up and walked out. There was such confusion and turmoil over that that a recess was called and I went to find out where the hell they were. I found them in a room at the Statler. They were saying good-by to one another, they were in tears, they were broken, they were going home because they felt nobody had left with them. I asked them to give me an opportunity to go back [to the GA] and ask for the right to speak. I went to Joe Fisher and asked for a point of personal privilege to tell the delegates what was happening to our black members. . . . I said that I'm going over to Arlington Street Church and I'd be glad to have any of you who want to join me so we can consider what we can do about this. And as I walked off the podium, one of my honored colleagues got up and spit in my face.

Passions ran so high that not only friendships but families were torn apart. Marcia McBroom, African American director of religious education at New York's Community Church, was standing in line wearing her BAWA button to register for the Boston General Assembly when the man in front of her turned around. It was her father, wearing an equally prominent BUUC badge. The encounter became so heated that Donald Harrington, her minister, offered to let her go home, but she stuck it out.

Another black Community Church delegate, Betty Bobo Seiden, attributes her negative views of BAC to two experiences: "The first shock was to discover [at the Cleveland GA] that so many of the African American delegates were not Unitarian Universalists. As one of them told me when I asked him about his church, 'What church? I'm here for the money.'" The second shock, in Boston the next year, "was witnessing the violation of our UU principles . . . of justice and equity in human relationships." She remembers running to the platform when the BAC/FULLBAC delegations walked out "in order to show with my presence . . . that all that rhetoric about the black delegates leaving the denomination was not true. Some of us were still there. Some of us are still here, still searching for truth and meaning, hoping that we can do so together in community."

Nor did things calm down after the Boston GA. Lawrence Ladd, an LRY leader at the time and now the UUA's financial advisor, recalls arriving at a Board meeting in January 1970 to a scene "unparalleled at any past meetings." Newly elected President Robert West had moved the meetings, which used to be held in the privacy of the president's office, to a room where observers were welcome. According to Ladd, "The seats for observers were all filled, so that most of the . . . people lined the walls of the meeting room, surrounding the trustees and literally peering over their shoulders. . . . The tension of this drama mounted from the opening session until the final vote just before 5:00 p.m." And West recalls the day a television crew came to interview him and a BAC leader, having got wind of it, invaded his office and preempted the cameras, never giving West a chance to speak.

Perhaps it was such confrontations that Dwight Brown, former parish minister and district executive, recalls when he refers to the "flaming emotions which consumed all sides. " He voted for BAC funding in Cleveland but not the next year because he felt that BAC's intransigence was hurting rather than helping their cause. And Max Gaebler, minister emeritus of the Madison, Wisconsin, church, still insists that BAC's tactics were a "deliberate attempt to polarize . . . completely abandoning rational discussion."

On the other hand, Winifred Norman, while conceding that "to divide the denomination is never a good thing, if this was the only way to shake us up to understand what the issues were, I'd say it *was* a good thing."

Ladd adds an interesting perspective. "The motivation for BAC supporters, certainly for young people," he suggests, "was in part a reaction to the coldness and sterility they saw in the denomination. The Black Affairs Council symbolized a reaction against its overly rational emphasis—'God's frozen people' in that famous phrase—and stood for a desire for greater spirituality, more emotion, and a greater sense of commitment."

And Homer Jack, who was at the center of the storm as head of the UUA department that convened the Biltmore conference, wound up stating that he still believed in Black Power "but not in the antics of its supporters, white and black, in our denomination." Indeed, at one point he called their tactics "fascist."

A 1970 sermon at Arlington Street Church that Jack quotes in his autobiography, reflects the same ambivalence: "The uneasy tranquility of our liberal denomination was broken by caucuses, name-calling, walkouts, microphone occupation. . . . [Yet] our learning about race relations has never been greater. Our wounds have never been deeper. Our denomination will never be the same again because of this racial agony." In many ways it was also a personal agony for him. Compelled both by his official position and by inner inclination to try to bridge an unbridgeable gap, he found himself taking abuse from all sides. In 1969, he left the UUA staff when his department was abolished as part of the headquarters consolidation. (He said he was fired.) Continuing as secretary general of the World Conference on Religion and Peace until 1984, he returned to the parish ministry. A good clue to both his fierce commitments and his personality comes in the heading of the chronological summary at the end of his autobiography. He calls it "Honors, Awards, and Arrests."

LOOKING BACK

Even after all these years, just asking the participants in the BAC/BAWA controversy for their recollections is apt to arouse all the old antagonisms. The only thing they seem able to agree on is that no compromise was possible. So is there a summing up? The trouble is that there's not one; there are many—almost as many as there are recollections. Let us consider only two, both from people deeply involved from the beginning of the controversy but on opposite sides of the issue.

Jeanette Hopkins chaired one of the four study commissions at the Biltmore conference. As she recalls, "I knew from the moment I arrived that there was going to be trouble. The radical blacks from Los Angeles were accorded double representation when they registered, as if they were equivalent to two people." Also, Robert's Rules of Order were applied selectively: "It was the height of white condescension and paternalism. It was also a cynical effort to control the outcome."

What upset her most was the pressure brought to bear on black people who had been long-time members of UU churches to make them join the Black Caucus: "They were ostracized and criticized in the most horrifying way." When the meeting divided along racial lines, Hopkins resigned, issuing a statement that read in part, "The conference . . . seems to be alien to the Unitarian Universalist movement. . . . If this is the best we can offer, [we] face the possibility of being judged irrelevant in this time."

And that is what, still today, she considers the great tragedy of the controversy:

> Obviously there was total racial injustice in our country, and still is. But we, who ought to have been the most sophisticated on matters related to racial justice, instead took a position that was both naïve and cynical. We were patronizing and paternalistic, betraying the blacks who had all along been members of our churches. They were treated like dirt, and that's part of the reason we have never done what we should have to integrate our churches. . . . We, who should have been a model in the fight against racial injustice, instead spent our energies fighting among ourselves.

That's one side of the story. The other is represented by the equally deeply felt conviction of Norma Poinsett, who has been one of the black members of the First Unitarian Church of Chicago for more than forty years, became a member-at-large of the UUA Board of Trustees, and also served on the Commission on Appraisal for part of the time it was studying the black empowerment controversy. She voted for BAC funding at the Cleveland General Assembly and still feels strongly that the BAC initiative was constructive.

Says Poinsett looking back, "There are so many interpretations as to why the denomination got cold feet at the Seattle GA. Some say it was financial problems; some say it was the issue about audit reports. I still believe that they really didn't like the idea of black people deciding what to do with the money. The denomination felt that it was a 'nice' thing to do, maybe even the right thing to do [to support BAC], but they didn't want to be inconvenienced by it."

Then, oddly echoing the comment by Betty Seiden, someone on the other side, she adds, "I didn't leave. I stayed on. I knew enough about the UUA to understand some of the frustrations, that everything moves so slowly, that you don't change minds that fast. Anyway, I wasn't a Unitarian Universalist because I thought they were non-racist. I was a member because of what the religion means to me." And she feels vindicated in staying on. "I think now we've come closest to doing the right thing. The anti-racism workshops all around this country have helped not only local churches but the whole tone of the Association, including the General Assemblies. Yes, we still have far to go, but everything is much fairer."

That hopeful note is echoed by Melvin Hoover, director of Faith in Action, who said about the current antiracist efforts, "We have been provided with that rarest of human opportunities— a second chance."

PAYING THE PRICE FOR FREEDOM

I call that mind free which jealously guards its intellectual rights and powers.

William Ellery Channing, no. 592

Robert West was not naïve about the financial situation of the UUA when he ran for president. A cartoon that circulated at the General Assembly that elected him showed him running the Association out of a phone booth. Even so, once he took office, he received a nasty shock.

West had spelled out in his platform his belief that "our movement today is in severe crisis affecting programs, finances, attitudes, and identity. There are issues so important and feelings of such intensity that some see our effectiveness, even our existence, as being seriously threatened."

Among the specific threats he mentioned were the turmoil surrounding the BAC/BAWA controversy and the financial situation: "The current year's $650,000 deficit in a budget of some $2,700,000—with almost all of our unrestricted capital gone— is an immediate crisis that must be faced."

Despite all the anger and confusion at the 1969 General Assembly, West received more votes than the other six candidates combined, so presumably the denomination wanted a healer and a centrist, thereby endorsing the key points in his platform:

- To fund the Black Affairs Council not through the denominational budget as the GA had voted, but through special voluntary campaigns.
- To improve communications by starting a newspaper to be sent to the homes of every UU member family. (Both the Unitarian and Universalist journals had always been subscription publications of minimal circulation.)
- To strengthen district operations so as to move program services nearer to congregations.
- And most critically, to address the financial crisis by asking, "What are the essential functions of our continental organization? What does the UUA *have* to do? What are our priorities? Let us identify three or four and proceed to perform them well."

The shock that awaited West came in January of 1970. He had taken office at the 1969 General Assembly, so that the fiscal year was already well under way, and having met with the finance committee, he thought that he had got on top of the situation. But at a board meeting that month an assistant treasurer told him, almost casually, that there was a demand note due for $450,000— and that the last $50,000 of that amount had been borrowed just two weeks before West took office. No one, however, had bothered to tell him about it either then or in the following months.

West met with the bankers as soon as he could, and by telling them of his plans to bring the budget into balance and to pay off the debt, got them to agree not to call the note. Bankruptcy had been avoided, but it was a near miss.

West was then thirty-nine, having previously served as parish minister in Knoxville, Tennessee, then in Rochester, New York. During the Greeley administration he had served as chair of the Advisory Committee to the Department of Education, and on a three-person committee to study the theological schools: Harvard, Meadville/Lombard, and Starr King. (Though Harvard was no longer a denominational school, it still trained a high percentage of UU ministers.) West had not planned to run for office, but the candidate he was supporting, Harry Scholefield of the San Francisco church, eventually decided that he would rather stay in the parish ministry.

West's plan to balance the budget was drastic. In addition to terminating the treasurer, he proposed, and the Board approved, consolidating the eight headquarters departments into five, funding seven interdistrict executives and offices instead of the existing twenty-one districts, reducing UUA staff from more than one hundred to fifty-five, and stretching out the funding of BAC by one year. All told, the budget cuts totaled $1 million—a full 40 percent. In addition, West pledged that no future budget would exceed the income that could be realistically expected, and that the bank loan would be repaid by applying all future unrestricted bequests to debt reduction and not, as had been the pattern, to current expenses. "My approach in devising the reorganization and budget reduction," West has said, commenting on his measures to restore the denomination to fiscal health, "was to focus on what I believed to be the primary purpose of the UUA: to serve the needs of local congregations . . . [and] to preserve and enhance those UUA programs and services that were most likely to help congregations with basic needs."

It was radical surgery, and it did not make Bob West popular with those who lost their jobs, hated to see their district offices closed, or did not fully understand the necessity. In retrospect, however, those who knew the situation have credited West with saving the denomination. Several of them, including Alan Deale, have independently called him "the unsung hero of the UUA." And as Carl Scovel says, "Dana left Bob with a horrible job . . . pulling this organization back into manageable size. What a terrible job! Firing people, closing down district programs. I have a great deal of respect for Bob West."

But West also understood that cutting budgets, while necessary in the short run, would not solve the denomination's basic problems. He, in Deale's words, "was scurrying around the country, trying desperately to raise more money and save the show." And it worked. By his sixth year in office, after ever-declining contributions going back to the Greeley years, the UUA Annual Program Fund, despite a fairly severe national recession, finally

began to recover, increasing by a modest but significant 4.3 percent in 1974-1975 over the year before. That, however, was only
the second prong of West's three-fold strategy for putting the
financial house in order. The third was to obtain funding from
the Veatch program of what is now the UU Congregation at Shelter Rock, New York. In that, too, he was successful, but the
Veatch story is so critical in the denomination's history that it
deserves to be told separately.

AN ERA OF ILL FEELING

West recalls that anti-institutionalism was another major problem when he took office, perhaps only second to the financial
crisis. "Supposedly responsible UU ministers were publishing
such sentiments as 'UUA headquarters should be blown up,'" he
recalls, or that "'25 Beacon Street should be sunk in Boston Harbor.'" Other ministers compared West to Nixon, and observers
at UUA board meetings were yelling insults at the members while
they were trying to conduct business.

Such behavior was not unique to Unitarian Universalists. It
was a time when confrontation, rudeness, and worse were considered signs of moral superiority. For example, when E.O.
Wilson, who pioneered the concept of biodiversity, was giving a
lecture at a scientific meeting, a protester, angered by something
Wilson had said in his book on *Sociobiology,* stormed the platform, grabbed the pitcher of ice water, and poured it over Wilson's
head. What's indicative of the temper of the times is that such
actions were widely hailed and emulated by those who were
rather glibly talking about the need for revolution. It was a time
when liberalism was denounced not only by the McCarthyite/
Nixonite Right but also by the radical Left, succeeding in demo-
nizing the "L Word" for a generation to come.

After all the dissension caused by the BAC/BAWA controversy,
draft card burning, and the sanctuary movement, "there was,"
as West puts it, "not enough of a sense of *we* in our denomination." Even when Dana Greeley had joined anti-war protests in
the 1960s, he felt forced to acknowledge that "there are widely

varying views in my denomination." And Jack Mendelsohn, minister of Arlington Street Church, where hospitality to the protest movement had made it in his words "the most notorious and celebrated UU congregation in the USA," realized that "there were people who considered what we did to be treason." As demonstrated by the letters column of the denominational journal, some of those who shared this sentiment were fellow Unitarian Universalists.

At first, most Unitarian Universalists stood somewhere in the middle—opposed to the Vietnam War but unwilling to join in civil disobedience. William Schulz, for instance, before the shooting of the Kent State students radicalized him, had opposed the action of his fellow students at Antioch when they built blockades to keep armed forces recruiters from entering the campus. And while he had the solid support of his church members for the memorial service he conducted in honor of the murdered students, when he proposed that the church join many others in the denomination in refusing to pay their telephone tax—a tax specifically enacted to help fund the war—the motion squeaked through by just one vote.

Having spoken out forcefully against the war as parish minister in Rochester, West was, like Greeley, firm in his own convictions but careful not to go beyond official General Assembly positions when speaking for the association. When a major anti-war rally was held on Boston Common across from 25 Beacon Street, he decided to show support by hanging a four-story banner from the front of the building, but chose as its message a quote from a GA resolution: "The Unitarian Universalist Association transmits to the President and Congress its continued concern for peace in Vietnam"—words a bit more circumspect than those of anti-war demonstrators whose chants called Lyndon Johnson a baby killer and Ho Chi Minh a hero.

Enter Mr. Nixon.

Having defeated Hubert Humphrey in the 1968 election and won again in 1972, he now sought to destroy those on his "enemies list."

BEACON PRESS AND THE PENTAGON PAPERS

In the summer of 1971, Gobin Stair, director of Beacon Press, came to Bob West for approval to publish the Pentagon Papers. Earlier that year, Daniel Ellsberg, a former consultant to the Department of Defense, had made public the secret seven thousand-page collection of documents and analyses prepared by an internal Pentagon study group that documented the duplicity practiced by the government to get us into the war and maintain public support. When the *Washington Post* and the *New York Times* decided to publish excerpts, it drove Nixon crazy. Pleading national security, he tried unsuccessfully to get the courts to suppress publication; when that failed he turned the notorious White House "plumbers" loose to find out how the leak had occurred.

Mike Gravel was then one of two Unitarian Universalist members of the United States Senate. "Someone called me on the phone," he recalled. "Later I found out it was Ellsberg himself, but at the time he wouldn't identify himself. I was filibustering the draft and he asked whether I would read the papers into the record and I said yes. [Even] George McGovern, who later ran for President on an anti-war platform, had refused to touch this stuff."

The papers were then turned over to Gravel by Ben Bagdikian of the *Washington Post,* who incidentally was also a Unitarian Universalist. "I met him at midnight under the marquee of the Mayflower Hotel in the heart of Washington," Gravel's reminiscence continues. "His car was parked and I pulled up abreast of his car. He opened his trunk, tossed the papers in my trunk, and I sped away. He had suggested we do it in the dark in some suburb, but I had once been a counter-intelligence officer and I said the hell with that—that's just inviting somebody to frag you." (*Frag* was soldiers' jargon for killing people—such as unpopular officers in Vietnam—by tossing a fragmentation bomb into their tents.)

Anyone who didn't live through those years might question the need for Gravel's cloak-and-dagger tactics. Keep in mind that this was the time when Nixon encouraged the "hard hats" to rough up peaceful demonstrators, when his plumbers broke into the office of Ellsworth's psychiatrist looking for incriminating information in his medical records, and a short time later also broke into Democratic offices at the Watergate. Paranoia was in the air, and not without reason.

Senator Gravel wanted the papers because he felt that publication of the full document in book form was essential for the historical record. However, he was turned down by some three dozen publishers. "They were just afraid," he recalls. Then he thought Beacon Press might be interested and he met with Gobin Stair. "We went forward from there. As a UU myself," he sums up, "I was just so proud to be associated with the Unitarian Universalist Association in this undertaking."

Stair did not hesitate. "The *Times* edition," he felt, "did not do justice to the original. . . . It was essential to make the full record available, especially to scholars, and as a free press we felt we had a responsibility to publish needed information when others would not." West not only backed him up but, in a statement to the denomination, put the decision in a broader context: "The issue is whether the American public has the role of central participant in the democratic process, or passive observer of government actions."

A VISIT FROM THE FBI

The UUA soon had a close-up view of government actions. First, on October 10, 1971, the Pentagon rushed its own heavily censored version into print, stealing Beacon's thunder by twelve days. So sudden was their effort that they reproduced raw, even illegible documents, skipping such editorial niceties as page numbers. As Gravel commented, "Clearly the Pentagon version was intended to sabotage our publication, and it did have that effect in the short run, but by coming out with their own they admitted that there were no national security secrets. It exposed the hypocrisy of the government."

More was to come.

On October 27, FBI agents appeared at the UUA's bank asking to see the Association's records. No one would even have known about this snooping expedition if a bank vice president, acting on his own initiative, had not called the UUA treasurer. When the bank then insisted on seeing a subpoena, the government got a grand jury to order the bank to turn over all checks drawn on and deposited in UUA accounts between June 1 and October 1. The next day, the FBI agents came back to "assist" bank employees in responding to the subpoena.

William Duffy of the UUA's law firm at the time has said, "It was a very frightening time. The government was using grand jury investigations to intimidate people who were resisting the war, so publication of the Pentagon Papers was a highly courageous act that risked criminal sanctions." Or as Bob West puts it, "Bill Duffy explained to me that it was his job to keep Gobin and me out of jail."

Gravel and the UUA went to court and secured a ruling ordering a temporary halt to the FBI investigations. Nonetheless, FBI agents tried again to obtain the UUA's records, and only when Gravel started contempt proceedings against the government did the Justice Department suspend the search. Eventually the case went all the way to the Supreme Court, which ruled that Gravel had immunity but that Beacon Press did not. This would have freed the administration once again to go after the UUA, but by this time the unfolding of the Watergate scandal meant that Nixon and his plumbers had more pressing concerns.

As for Gravel, though his initiatives ended his political career, he has said, "I would do it again in a flash. It was very distressing to recognize that the American publishing empires had no guts to do what was right—to inform the people in a democracy. It was very worthwhile doing."

Within the denomination, there was virtually no dissent. Supporting statements came from UU congregations everywhere, and West found solid support in his speech-making tours of the country, explaining what had happened. (He also found, however, great anxiety that local congregations, too, might be investigated.) Even critics of his administration like Jack Mendelsohn spoke out in support. "It took some guts on Bob's part," Mendelsohn has said, "to do what he did."

The UUA Board, though realizing that each member individually might become the target of FBI harassment, unanimously adopted a resolution that said in part, "For the first time in the history of our country, the Federal government is attempting to subpoena the financial records of a national religious organization, including the names of its members and contributors. . . . The Board of Trustees of the Unitarian Universalist Association is determined to resist this unwarranted and unconstitutional attack."

The UUA's action also won wide public support. Said *The New York Times*, "The Government's harassment of Beacon Press . . . imperils not only press freedom but constitutional rights involving religion and association as well." Gobin Stair sees a direct link between the UUA's stand and Nixon's resignation: "We helped to change the thinking about the actions of the Administration. . . . It was a watershed event in the denomination's history and a high point in Beacon's fulfilling its role as a public pulpit for proclaiming Unitarian Universalist principles."

Like so much of history, it all seems so obvious in retrospect, but these were not easy decisions at the time, for while the government could not chill Unitarian Universalist commitment to freedom of the press and the democratic process, they could, and did, cause the UUA great harm by making it incur endless legal expenses that once again put the Association's finances in jeopardy. Again Veatch funds came to the rescue—part of an extraordinary story of denominational support.

TURNING THE TIDE

Despite these tribulations and distractions, the West administration was marked by several achievements that—in calmer times—would have been considered noteworthy.

Among several new curriculum kits developed in those years was *Human Sexuality*, later called *About Your Sexuality*, the groundbreaking teaching program that had its origins in West's Rochester congregation, and was the predecessor to today's

Our Whole Lives program. It was the first time a religious denomination had dared to tackle this delicate subject honestly, with an emphasis on being helpful to kids rather than on using scare tactics to maintain traditional rules of behavior.

West, following up on a General Assembly vote, also established the first Office of Gay Concerns and hired its director. A little later, a full-time administrative secretary—all the budget could support—was added to head an Office on Aging. Nor were the needs of children overlooked. The UUA produced public service announcements on child abuse and offered them to TV stations around the United States free of charge. West failed, however, in another attempt to get the Service Committee to combine with the UUA Department of Social Responsibility. The UUA Board supported him but the UUSC Board did not.

What he did succeed in doing was to introduce professional management at UUA headquarters. He appointed Robert Senghas, trained as a lawyer as well as a minister, as his executive vice president. According to Senghas, by the time he joined the staff West had already brought in a professional personnel advisor, graded all jobs, and established firm salary ranges, putting an end to a system where staff members negotiated with the president behind closed doors for the best deal each could get. The new administration also put an end to off-budget expenditures, which had kept even the board from a full understanding of the financial situation, and—since many of the money problems were due to the deficits run up by Beacon Press—Beacon was brought under the administrative (but not editorial) jurisdiction of the UUA Board. Until then, the press had been run by an independent board even though the Association had to pick up the bills.

But perhaps the innovation that remains most visible today is the launch of the *Unitarian Universalist World* (now *UU World*), which began publication in March 1970 as a tabloid newspaper that was mailed to the homes of sixty thousand UU families free of charge, using money that had previously gone to subsidize the subscription magazine. This had been one of West's primary platform planks: to create a medium for timely communication between headquarters and all members of local congregations. It made the existence of the UUA real to Unitarian Universalists in a way that had never been attempted before, and also made it possible to share news of what other congregations and districts were doing, building a new sense of denominational identity and belonging.

This new sense of belonging was undoubtedly one factor—along with Nixon's unintended help—in uniting the denomination and stopping many years of attrition in membership. As a consequence of compiling the *UU World's* mailing list, there was for the first time an accurate way to assess total membership. Previously, the membership numbers submitted by the local congregations had often been inflated; now congregations were asked to submit actual names. This switch has made it impossible to determine whether the shrinkage of the early 1970s was factitious or real. For example, one congregation that had been reporting five thousand members in its UUA Directory listing was found to have a regular Sunday attendance of less than one hundred. Also, LRY membership was no longer included in the national membership total.

Furthermore, West launched a "Sharing in Growth" program that focused not only on membership extension but on reinforcing the depth of programs and individual commitment. During the last two years of his term, not only did membership figures begin to show an upswing, but the Annual Fund, as mentioned, also showed an increase, meeting its goal for the first time in about a decade.

Another of West's decisions that proved important in the life of the denomination was to create a new position in the Department of the Ministry to deal exclusively with theological education and to recruit as its head O. Eugene Pickett, minister in Atlanta, Georgia, and a personal friend. Pickett had seen his congregation grow from 300 when he arrived to 1,150 when he left twelve years later, with an average Sunday attendance of 850. Pickett would later serve as UUA president, an unlikely development had he not been on the headquarters staff when his predecessor died in office.

In 1975, further budget cuts led to the consolidation of five program departments into one, and West appointed Pickett to head the new Department of Ministerial and Educational Services. The anger he encountered trying to explain this change to groups of ministers and district leaders made him wonder, as described in Tom Owen-Towle's biography, whether there wasn't an easier way to make a living.

Reflecting on this period in the life of the UUA, Pickett was to say: "Bob West became President during one of the most difficult periods in the life of the Association. He had to overcome tremendous obstacles to keep [it] solvent while keeping it operating— and it operated at a surprising degree of effectiveness. . . . Bob was a strong, competent administrator and exceedingly conscientious about being on top of every detail of the operation."

West himself was gratified to observe an encouraging change in mood in the denomination: "In contrast to the early seventies, a dominant tone of optimism and hope seemed to have developed, together with a level of vitality that had not existed then. There was a constructive climate among lay people and clergy; the morale of ministers was much higher; people seemed to feel that problems were solvable." Also, he sensed that "there was a renewed interest in worship and theology . . . [and] a renewed interest in personal religious growth and depth in personal religion."

Unfortunately, the struggles of his eight-year presidency (he had been reelected for a second term without opposition) took their toll on him personally: "By the time I arrived at 25," Pickett told Owen-Towle, "he seemed to me to be worn down, experiencing minimal enjoyment or satisfaction from the job. It was my impression that he was feeling very much alone— unsupported and unappreciated."

No wonder. He had faced harsh criticism and unbelievable vituperation. When his term ended, he spent a sabbatical in England and then joined the private sector. In fact, both he and the moderator, Joseph Fisher, had seriously discussed not running again in 1973 because the experience was so stressful and unpleasant; they changed their minds only out of a sense of obligation to a denomination that seemed intent on tearing itself apart and would be further divided by a presidential contest. Almost everyone compliments West and Fisher from the vantage of hindsight, but their work was not widely appreciated when support was most needed. Let one final compliment speak for all the others. Gordon McKeeman, who served on the UUA board with West, credits him with "doing all the right things with courage and caring and with finesse and grace." Coming from one of the UUA's most distinguished retired ministers—himself twice a candidate for the presidency—that says it all.

VEATCH TO THE RESCUE

We lift our hearts in thanks today.
Percival Chubb, no. 355

Although it didn't yet exist, February 10, 1945, was a red letter day for the Unitarian Universalist Association. This was the day the North Shore Unitarian Society (now named the Unitarian Universalist Congregation at Shelter Rock) in New York's Nassau County was incorporated. Eventually, the congregation was to come into a great deal of money, money that with astonishing generosity it agreed to share with social causes reflecting its religious ideals and with the UUA. As President John Buehrens has summed up in a 1993 letter to the Shelter Rock congregation, "You have literally saved the UUA as an organization, revitalized our social witness, dramatically strengthened our efforts in ministerial training, made possible creative new programs, and funded much of what we have accomplished in recent years to grow and extend Unitarian Universalism." In light of that record, it is worth telling the "Veatch story" in some detail.

The prime movers in the founding of the North Shore congregation were four young couples who had formed the Port

Washington Unitarian Sunday School Committee in 1941. "In this time of national crisis," their statement of purpose read, "it is more important than ever to remember the spiritual needs of the growing generation. . . . In the world of tomorrow, as well as in this critical time, our children need the teachings of a liberal religion if they are to understand their responsibilities in a world dedicated to freedom for all peoples." The story of the founding is eloquently told by Robert Sunley, a Shelter Rock member and historian, in a highly illustrated volume aptly called *We Started with the Children.* As he reports, twenty children attended on opening day, and by 1945, when school attendance had grown to forty-five, the adults decided to form a Unitarian society. At first they met in the local American Legion hall, but by the fall of their first year they were in a position to purchase their first piece of property. It cost only $8,750, but even so they were able to afford it only because the American Unitarian Association gave them a building loan of $4,500, together with a subsidy of $1,200 toward the salary of their new minister, Gerald F. Weary. Rarely has an investment paid richer dividends.

Anxious to make their bold enterprise viable, the leaders of the new society made up a list of non-Unitarian community residents who might be willing to make a one-time contribution. One of the members, Julia Wagner, had been giving physical therapy to a well-off, homebound woman who, she thought, was worth adding to the list. The woman's name was Caroline (Carrie) Veatch. She had been widowed since 1938 and was living with her sister. As Weary tells the story in *A Memorial to Caroline E. Veatch,* she made a generous contribution and he made a follow-up call on the two sisters before he even conducted his first service. Weary writes, "One of Carrie's two house helpers answered the door," and took him to the second floor where each sister had her own apartment. "Carrie did not rise to greet me; she was obviously an invalid. [She had injured her back in a riding accident.] She wore a white blouse, with a brooch at the collar, and her hair was parted, and combed back. . . . Though I detected some sadness and tiredness in her face and voice, I sensed at once that she was a person of poise and dignity, and as well, of warmth and friendliness."

For the next eight years, until Carrie died, Weary and sometimes his wife called on her at least every other week. Gradually he heard the story of her husband's explorations in northern Germany, where salt domes led him, as a world famous oil geologist, to assume that drilling might prove successful. Securing promising concessions, he became a major stockholder in the North European Oil Corporation; the Great Depression of the 1930s, however, forced the company to sell its holdings to major international oil companies, a deal that left Veatch in possession of promising—but at the time non-producing—royalty rights, plus some remaining stock.

Thanks to Weary's visits, the sisters had begun to express an interest in the North Shore Unitarian Society. Being an invalid, Carrie was unable to attend church activities, but Weary had put the sisters on the society's mailing list, so they were well informed about its growth and activities and read his sermons with great interest. After about two years of Weary's faithful visits, he recalls, she "initiated a conversation with me about remembering the Society in her will." Three years later she brought up the question of her (still non-producing) royalty rights.

A FATEFUL FRIENDSHIP

By now the sisters had begun making gifts both of cash and of furniture for the original meeting house, and as the society kept growing, Carrie wrote a $2,500 check toward the new, larger building when the congregation moved from its original home in Port Washington, New York, to larger quarters in Plandome. (It has since relocated once again, to Manhasset.) When Carrie read about the society's fund-raising drive to help the suffering Unitarians in Czechoslovakia, she came through with another check, and also contributed to the Unitarian Service Committee. "When Carrie told me that she wanted to make a bequest to our society," Weary writes, "I felt the time had come when I could ask her whether she would like to become a member . . . and she said she would. On March 28, 1948, I took the membership book to her and she signed it." As for the bequest, she explained that she wanted to help assure what she saw as the Unitarians' "splendid future," but since that would require rewriting her will, she asked Weary to recommend an attorney. She also needed help, she added, to obtain the oil royalties that were gradually beginning to accumulate in Germany. If he succeeded, she promised, she would give half to the North Shore Society.

Getting the money was no easy task. Records had been lost in the war; corporations made conflicting claims, but after two years James Nickerson, the attorney Weary had recruited from his congregation, was able to report success. "On January 14, 1952, Jim [Nickerson] received from Germany a remittance in United States dollars of $7,168, and turned it over to Carrie who, in turn, by her agreement with me, gave one-half to the North Shore Unitarian Society." Feeling that after sharing two more remittances she had fulfilled her obligation, Weary decided he had better ask her whether she, indeed, wanted the split to continue as long as she lived. When she said yes, he added a second question: whether upon her death she would leave her royalty rights to the society.

She said yes again.

On November 10—maybe that's another red letter day—an agreement to this effect was signed and notarized, and when Carrie Veatch died of cancer on October 4, 1953, the will went into effect. At first the income generated by the bequest was modest, but even the $40,000 a year it generated at the start made for a welcome supplement to the congregation's budget.

UNEXPECTED RICHES

Then two things happened. Robert Adelman, an attorney member of the congregation and its president from 1968 to 1970, was instrumental in getting the United States–West German tax treaty amended so that Veatch income was no longer taxable in Germany. That literally doubled the amount of Veatch revenues.

The second was that natural gas was discovered in the German oil fields. From then on, the amounts received by the congregation began to grow explosively.

There is nothing like unexpected riches to bring out someone's true character. Take lottery winners. Some salt the extra income away for a rainy day while others spend it all on themselves; sometimes families tear themselves apart in passionate squabbles. Rarely do they find creative ways to help others. What is true of lottery winners is also true of religious congregations, but right from the beginning, the North Shore Unitarian Society opted for generosity and vision. While Veatch income was still modest, the congregation would lend $1,000 to one sister Unitarian church for new lights, or give $500 to another for bridge tables. That was followed by small building loans to fellow congregations. By 1958, Veatch bequest proceeds had risen to the point that the congregation voted to keep only 75 percent for itself and give 25 percent away. As still more money came in, they reversed these percentages. Soon the board found that making all these decisions was too time-consuming and that a more structured system was called for. In 1959 the Caroline Veatch Assistance and Extension Program was launched. The operative "whereas" of the congregational resolution read: "It is thought that the establishment of a program for existing Unitarian Fellowships and Churches and other Unitarian programs through loans and/or gifts which are designed to foster and promote Unitarianism will be a worthy program in its own right and one which will suitably and appropriately honor Caroline Veatch."

This action was taken two years before the formation of the UUA. The first recorded support of the UUA was a loan of $500 in 1962. In 1965, another small chunk of money went to the UU United Nations Office. In 1969, a subsequent congregational resolution resolved that "In making grants and/or loans, Unitarian Universalist Association programs, both local and continental should receive first consideration at all times." It was a resolve that resulted in many gifts to the UUA and other UU causes, including

- a 1970 emergency loan for working capital.
- funding for development of religious education curricula.
- grants to the Racial Justice Fund and other social concerns commitments.
- paying the legal costs associated with publication of the Pentagon Papers.
- encouraging denominational giving by matching the contributions of other congregations to the Annual Program Fund, culminating in the establishment of a $20-million UUA endowment trust fund and annual subsidies for the UUA grants program.
- subsidies for ministerial salaries and pensions.
- a building loan fund.
- and just to prove how comprehensive and imaginative their support could be, $6,000 for the "troubadour ministry" of Ric Masten, a poet and singer, and an equal amount for the Chicago Children's Choir.

That's only a partial list. Meanwhile, Veatch support was also going to the Service Committee, to the UN office, to the IARF, to the New York Metropolitan District and its Long Island Area Council, to the Church of the Larger Fellowship, to individual UU congregations and summer camps, and to the Unitarian Theological Academy of Transylvania. An equally impressive list could be drawn up of gifts, grants, and loans to socially progressive community organizations. One technical point worth clearing up: Not all the money came from the Veatch Program. On many occasions, such as the grant for theological education, the congregation augmented the Veatch allocations with additional grants and gifts from its own budget.

None of this might have happened if Robert West, as soon as he assumed the UUA presidency, had not worked assiduously to develop a relationship of trust with the congregation. To assure them that the Association's finances were now being handled in a responsible and business-like manner, he invited Eleanor Vendig, the program administrator of what was then called the Veatch Committee (later dubbed the Veatch Board), to sit in on UUA board meetings as an observer. Together with her late husband and Alan Doran, Vendig had not only been one of the society's founders, but had been an architect of the Veatch program concept. What's more, we also owe much of the documentation about the program's development to her 1973 report titled "The Caroline Veatch Assistance and Extension Program: An Overview."

A further assurance that their funds were being put to good use came in 1973 when Robert Adelman was elected as the UUA's financial advisor, making him a voting member of the Board. Having been created in 1967 by action of a General Assembly alarmed by the profligacy of the Greeley administration, the position now became a vital link between the Association and the Veatch program.

Meanwhile Edward Lawrence, another active church member, had become chair of the Veatch Committee. "Ed and I used to commute together," Adelman recalls, "and I kept after him to make the grants bigger. 'Let's not buy new card tables—let's really make a difference.' Gradually it got to the point where you needed more than a committee. You needed an executive director. We got Ed to take that on after he retired, at first on a part-time basis, and we got Eleanor Vendig a full-time church job to keep all the records, and the two of them worked together for nearly twenty years."

Meanwhile the Veatch income got larger and larger, reaching almost $20 million in its peak year.

It was a situation that began to worry some members of the congregation. As the UUA's financier, they felt, they were in effect making policy and even management decisions for the entire denomination. There was also a concern, as Ed Lawrence has put it, that the congregation's board, which had to review all the recommendations of the Veatch committee, "was spending its time giving away money instead of running a church." After the initial decision to match contributions to the Annual Fund, a solution to both problems was worked out—a solution that would also protect the denomination against the possibility that at some point the natural gas money might run out. The answer was to set up an endowment trust fund for the UUA, which was completed in 1985 with the transfer totaling $20 million. The annual income, it was calculated, would match the Veatch funding the UUA had been receiving up to then, while removing the congregation from any role in deciding how the income should be spent.

POWERED BY NATURAL GAS

In December 1980, the North Shore congregation voted an additional grant of $120,000 a year—later raised to $200,000—to be allocated by a panel to be appointed by the UUA Board. In the first eight years, 143 programs were funded, including extension programs, religious education materials, and by way of example on the local level, publication of a tabloid newspaper sponsored by Arizona and Nevada congregations. Money was also allocated for historical research, a worship anthology called *Women's Words,* and an AIDS outreach ministry.

To an astonishing extent, the denomination's activities are— to quote the bumper sticker on utility company trucks—still powered by natural gas. In the 2000 fiscal year, for instance, combined Shelter Rock and Veatch grants totaled $1.9 million, making up 28 percent of the UUA operating budget. The year before, according to its 1999 report, the Veatch-supported Unitarian Universalist Funding Program approved grants totaling $825,705 that supported the work of social justice, strengthened UU institutions, made the UU faith more visible in the world, and encouraged generous support of the denomination. The report takes more than twenty printed pages just to list all the activities and organizations the funding program sustains and often makes possible. It is administered through three funds: for Unitarian Universalism, for social responsibility, and for a just society.

In addition, the Veatch Board of Governors still supports UU organizations not funded by the Association's budget, such as the theological schools.

One point that needs to be stressed, however, is that in putting its financial house in order with all the help it received from

Veatch and the Shelter Rock Congregation, the UUA did not ne-glect its efforts to become self-supporting. President Eugene Pickett took two vital steps to shore up the institution. He ini-tiated Friends of the UUA, an ongoing campaign to raise funds from individual Unitarian Universalists in addition to the fair share support their congregations are expected to give, and he launched the first post-consolidation capital campaign; called Visions for Growth, it ran from 1983 to 1987 and raised about $4 million. Each of Picket's successors since then has also added to the association's endowment. William Schulz began the Handing on the Future campaign in 1992, which raised more than $13.6 million in pledges by the time it was completed under his successor, John Buehrens, who in turn is ending his term while a campaign for $32 million—the Campaign for Unitarian Universalism—is under way.

By the mid-1970s the UUA's long shakedown cruise was over. At last the leadership would be able to concentrate on the UUA's true mission, the advancement of Unitarian Universalist religious ideals, rather than having to worry about keeping the enterprise from foundering. As the bylaws say, the Association's primary purpose is "to serve the needs of its member congregations, organize new congregations, extend and strengthen Unitarian Universalist institutions, and implement its principles." Fortu-nately, in the years that followed there were fewer crises to inter-fere with these objectives, enabling the denomination to develop a new, more coherent sense of identity.

Preserving the Future

NEW SYMBOLS, WORDS, AND SONGS

If they offer something better, I will gladly learn.
Francis David, no. 566

After its first sixteen not always easy years, the Unitarian Universalist Association seemed to take a metaphorical deep breath and enter into a period of greater confidence and stability, with renewed awareness of Unitarian Universalist values and potential.

But the UUA was to suffer one more blow before it was able to regain its forward momentum—the death of its president.

Paul Carnes had been minister in Buffalo, New York, and had considered running for the presidency in 1969 with Robert West's encouragement, but a bout with lymphoma ruled that out and instead he became West's campaign manager. By 1977, his illness in remission, he did run in a three-way race and won. A gifted speaker (his mother had predicted that he would end up a Methodist bishop), he had spent twenty-nine months in World War II as a prisoner of war, then entered Harvard Divinity School where he became interested in Unitarianism.

Tragically, after only about eighteen months in office, his cancer recurred. Carne's successor, Eugene Pickett—who had stayed on as head of the Department of Ministerial and Congregational Services—recalls walking into Carnes's office to find him staring at the wall over an empty desk. David Pohl, another staff member and a good friend, who later became head of the Department of Ministry, recalls Carnes saying, "'David, I don't know what I'm supposed to do here.' He was being funny, but it was also kind of plaintive."

There was also friction with the Board about Carnes's budget proposals. Particularly controversial were his wanting to close Starr King School for the Ministry and sell Beacon Press because of the financial drain they represented.

Even so, Carnes left his mark.

- He appointed a Commission on Worship that prepared the way for the formation of the Hymnbook Resources Commission.

- He established an office for affirmative action for women and African American ministers.

- He reestablished the Department of Social Responsibility and named William Schulz, later to become the fifth president of the UUA, as its head.

When Carnes died, it was up to the Board of Trustees to pick his successor, and there were two candidates: senior staff member Eugene Pickett and Gordon McKeeman, who along with Jack Mendelsohn had contested the 1977 election. McKeeman had been one of the young Universalist ministers who before consolidation had organized a group they called the Humiliati to breathe new life and new thought into their denomination. He then served on the UUA Board as his district's representative, and later as president of the UU Service Committee. McKeeman had considered himself "the non-political candidate," explaining that Carnes and Mendelsohn had been on opposite sides of the black power controversy, and "it seemed to me that these two candidates running against each other was going to be disastrous for the denomination." Also, he felt it was vitally important to preserve the Universalist identity, and by that time "the Universalists were beginning to think there will never be a Universalist president if we don't do something about it."

With about half the Board favoring McKeeman, it looked for a while as if the moderator would have to break a tie. In the event, however, Pickett won by a vote of fourteen to twelve and McKeeman went on to become president of Starr King School, the West Coast UU seminary.

The Pickett years were good years for the denomination and much was accomplished. But while the doings at "25" deserve attention, it is often the subtle, more hidden changes that define our denominational life. And as usual, outside influences had much to do with these changes.

Two seminal books that had appeared in the 1960s were chipping away at some stifling cultural assumptions. Michael Harrington's *The Other America* and Betty Friedan's *Feminine Mystique* demonstrated not only that the need to put faith into action to fight the consequences of poverty was as great as ever, but that one of the wrongs that needed righting was the historic suppression of women. To change perceptions even further, this was also the time when Microsoft was founded and the first Apple home computers hit the market. Suddenly it was time, the practitioners of the New Journalism assured us, for everything to be new: the New Age (including music and theology), the New Left, the new math, and because it's doubly chic in French, *nouvelle vague* movies, *nouveau romans* in literature, and tastiest of all, *nouvelle cuisine*.

What really was new were the mindsets of members seeking out UU congregations. No longer was the predominant stimulus rebellion against the orthodoxies of their youth; more likely they were in search of meaning in lives that had hitherto had no religious moorings.

Also changing was that most of the congregations they were joining were now designated Unitarian Universalist rather than either just Universalist or Unitarian.

NAMING THE BABY

It pays to think ahead when picking a name for a newborn what nickname he or she is likely to be saddled with. Either that didn't occur to the founders, who chose to call the new denomination the Unitarian Universalist Association, or since it was a compromise it simply wasn't their highest priority. There were some who still preferred Frederick May Eliot's approach of finding a totally different name, usually using such adjectives as "free" or "liberal," in hopes of attracting other faiths. The majority, however, wanted a name that maintained the historical connection with the predecessor denominations and gave them equal billing. That still left the question of which one should be mentioned first, and whether the two names should be connected by an "and" or a hyphen—or, as it turned out, nothing.

The Universalists, it was reported at the time, were delighted to be named second, making "Unitarian" grammatically an adjective. Even so, Dana Greeley questioned whether Unitarian Universalists should "go on endlessly trying to use the double name in common parlance." He felt, he says in his book, that while the dual designation should be kept in official documents, "we should be able to say that we are Universalists or that we are Unitarian," adding that "in the long run I think the Unitarian designation will prevail."

While wrong in that prediction, Greeley was quite right that the complicated name presented problems. Before consolidation, the Unitarian Laymen's League had been running small-space advertisements in selected newspapers and magazines with the heading "Are you a Unitarian without knowing it?" followed by a checklist of beliefs. These ads turned out to be highly successful in attracting members, who often formed the core of newly founded Fellowships. But when after consolidation the heading was changed to "Are you a Unitarian Universalist without knowing it?" the campaign had to be scrapped because it stopped working.

What Greeley did not anticipate was that the simplification that took place was the adoption of initials. Far from preserving both traditions, the law of unintended consequences determined that we managed to forfeit both by settling for a meaningless "UU." Yet even those who cringe at the unloveliness of that usage find that having said or written "Unitarian Universalist" more than twice in a row, they have little recourse but to say "UU." Many of our church banners and signboards say UU; there is even a minister who sports the license plate "UU REV."

While understandable, this bit of jargon is regrettable because the full name still has the power to inspire. *Unitarian* evokes a great historical and cultural tradition. *Universalist* for its part has powerful emotional resonance, for while universal salvation may not be much of a contemporary concern, many of the concepts that unite us—the interdependent web of all existence, the universality of humane values, the basic genetic unity of the human family—all are evoked by that one word *Universalist*. So perhaps Greeley's prediction that eventually we will settle for one name may still come true, but might it be "Universalist" rather than "Unitarian"? Dana would be shocked at the mere suggestion.

Meanwhile, it is striking as one looks down the list of our congregations in the Yearbook how many have incorporated "Unitarian Universalist" in their names or are using it as a kind of subhead. We are indeed a single entity and the original names do live on, even if not in what Greeley called "common parlance."

LIGHTING THE CHALICE

Nor is the name the only signifier of our identity; another is our widely used symbol, the flaming chalice, which actually predates consolidation but was not widely used before the founding of the UUA.

Hans Deutsch was an artist who had fled to Paris when Hitler invaded Austria and who, when the Germans conquered France, escaped from there to Spain and then to neutral Portugal. Also in Lisbon was Charles Joy, a Unitarian minister who had been sent to work with refugees and war victims as European commissioner of the newly founded Unitarian Service Committee (USC).

It was Joy's charge to help not only Czech Unitarians but also all others, primarily Jews, who were fleeing from the Nazis. Deutsch started working for the USC, and Joy asked him to design a symbol for the Committee that could be placed on its documents to make them look official and at the same time symbolize the nature of its work. As a new organization, the Service Committee lacked the identity that would give it credibility in those dangerous and chaotic times. As Dan Hotchkiss, the scholar/minister who has researched this subject, describes it in a UUA pamphlet, "This was . . . a cloak-and-dagger world, where establishing trust quickly across barriers of language, nationality, and faith could mean life instead of death. Disguises, signs and countersigns, and midnight runs across guarded borders were the means of freedom. . . ."

"When a document may keep a man out of jail, give him standing with the government and police, it is important that it look important," Joy explained in a 1941 letter to the USC executive director. He enclosed a sketch, and went on, "I have had it made up into a seal, not because I have any idea of forcing this upon the committee without consulting them, but because these things cost very little here, and at least will serve as a temporary expedient. . . . Personally, I like it very much. It is simple, chaste, and distinctive. I think it might well become the sign of our work everywhere. It represents, as you see, a chalice with a flame, the kind of chalice which the Greeks and Romans put on their altars. The holy oil burning in it is a symbol of helpfulness and sacrifice."

Apparently mindful not only of bureaucratic sensitivities but of the fact that he had recently lost the election for the AUA presidency in part because he was criticized for being too theistic, Joy went on to assure his bosses that the fact that the symbol "remotely suggests a cross was not in [the artist's] mind, but to me this also has its merit . . . [since] the cross does symbolize Christianity and its central theme of sacrificial love."

Deutsch certainly did not see it as a Christian symbol. As he later wrote to Joy, "I am not what you may actually call a believer. But if your kind of life is the profession of your faith—as it is, I feel sure—then religion, ceasing to be magic and mysticism, becomes confession to practical philosophy and—what is more—to active, really useful social work. And this religion—with or without a heading—is one to which even a 'godless' fellow like myself can say wholeheartedly, Yes!"

Wholeheartedly "yes" is most certainly what Unitarian Universalists have said ever since to the symbol Deutsch designed. His original sketch has been adapted in countless ways. Often, as by the UUA, it is combined with the double, slightly non-congruent circles that were intended to represent the two founding denominations; other versions retain the "off-center cross" that had been popular among Universalists. Some are more stylized, some less, but all hark back to the original concept, and its use has become ubiquitous. You see it on the letterheads of many congregations; on signboards; as pendants, pins, earrings, and other jewelry; on T-shirts; as wall hangings in places of worship; and on a striking number of the congregational banners carried at General Assembly opening parades. But perhaps most popular is the ceremonial lighting of the chalice that has become a common opening of UU Sunday services.

Here is just one example. The First Unitarian Church of Pittsburgh, Pennsylvania, recently held a ceremony dedicating its new flaming chalice. The minister, David Herndon, wrote in *First Days Record* that he led the congregation in a responsive reading that began, "We know that symbols alone do not make religion happen, but symbols can indeed remind us of our highest aspirations, our deepest commitments, and our most earnest intentions. . . . With its beauty and grace and strength, this new flaming chalice will remind us of our highest aspirations, our deepest commitments, and our most earnest intentions." The service then went on to pay tribute to Hans Deutsch, to the Unitarian Service Committee, and to Jan Hus, who was burned at the stake for challenging Christian orthodoxy by offering both the communion bread and wine to the laity, making the chalice a Hussite symbol. The Pittsburgh service also noted that the cross-like shape of their flaming chalice recalls the Christian roots of the Unitarian and Universalist traditions, while the fact that it is off-center serves as a reminder that no religious tradition can claim to be primary or exclusive.

The flaming chalice is now the official symbol of both the UUA and the Unitarian Universalist Service Committee, but its true genius is revealed by its spontaneous adoption by so many congregations and by the esteem in which it is so widely held. How fitting that it was created to further the Unitarian Service Committee's humanitarian effort by someone who, as Hotchkiss points out, "had never seen a Unitarian or Universalist church or heard a sermon. What he had seen was faith in action—people who were willing to risk all for others in a time of urgent need."

THE FLOWER COMMUNION

Another symbolic way of expressing our faith also came to us by way of Europe. At the annual flower communion observed by many congregations, members are asked to bring a blossom to the service, and after appropriate texts and music, each person is handed someone else's contribution. This popular ritual was developed by Norbert Čapek, who was for some twenty years minister of the Unitarian congregation in Prague. The author of three hymns and two readings in our hymnal, he died in a Nazi concentration camp, a martyr to his beliefs.

Incidentally, it wasn't until 2000 that the Prague congregation was able to return to its historic church, having been locked out for seven years in the aftermath of Communist oppression. To celebrate their return, according to Richard Boeke, a UU minister now living in England, the members conducted a flower communion attended by fellow Unitarians (there never having been many Universalists in Europe) from Denmark, Britain, and Germany. To quote a favorite Câpek hymn, number 28 in *Singing the Living Tradition*, "Trust that after winter's snowfall walls will melt and truth will flow."

PRINCIPLES AND PURPOSES

There are few issues about which Unitarian Universalists are not ambivalent but flowers and flames are sufficiently non-specific to permit us to accept them as appropriate symbols. It's tougher when it comes to words.

One thing we do all agree on: we refuse to accept a creed, defining creed as a statement we must accept to be members in good standing. But even as we vehemently reject any creed, we seem to be forever searching for some verbal formula to which we can all (or at least most of us) say, "Yes, that's what I (more or less) believe."

The importance of expressing the central core of the beliefs we share was well described by Eugene Pickett when he assumed the UUA presidency in 1979. Referring to the probems facing the denomination, Pickett said,

> The deeper malaise lies in our confusion as to what word we have to spread. The old watchwords of liberalism—freedom, reason, tolerance—worthy though they may be, are simply not catching the imagination of the contemporary world. They describe a process for approaching the religious depths but they testify to no intimate acquaintance with the depths themselves. If we are ever to speak to a new age, we must supplement our seeking with some profound religious finds.

The original Principles and Purposes of the Association no longer served that need. Adopted at the time of consolidation in 1960 after all-day, all-night negotiation and debate, the wording had come close to blowing up the whole consolidation process. Twenty years later they were barely remembered. It is a source of some amazement, therefore, that the new version that replaced them in 1984 was not only adopted overwhelmingly but, with a single addition, has remained unchanged for fifteen years. To a truly astonishing extent today's Principles and Purposes (we have taken to capitalizing them) have won a lasting place in UU hearts and been woven intimately into the fabric of our denominational life.

Here are just a few examples: They are featured in the front of our hymnbook—indeed, the commission that assembled the book took them "as the touchstones of our decision to proclaim our diversity." They have been widely reprinted in local congregations' orders of service, posted on church walls, even recited in unison. At the First Unitarian Congregation of Waterloo, Ontario, the Principles are the focus of each year's new members' recognition ceremony. As minister Anne Treadwell reported in *First Days Record*, the "responsibilities of membership can be summed up as a thoughtful commitment to the principles, and . . . making such a commitment can change lives." What's more, Judith Frediani, the UUA's director of curriculum development, points out that the Principles and Purposes were central in the effort to develop a religious education curriculum that both expresses and nurtures a UU sense of identity.

One final example. To make sure that the publishing efforts of Beacon Press were true to its mission as a public voice for Unitarian Universalist ideals, Wendy Strothman, while director of the press, required that her editors include with every editorial proposal a comment as to how that volume would support the UUA Principles and Purposes, a policy maintained by Helene Atwan, her current successor.

All this agreement, it is hardly necessary to add, does cause some discomfort among those who, while acknowledging that the "P&P" are not a creed in the dictionary sense, still see a common statement of belief that's quite so readily accepted as a sign of "creeping creedalism." Creeping or not, the process of reformulating our Principles proved amazingly amicable, and was in fact an outstanding example of covenanting—of maximum participation and dialogue, of total transparency, and of repeated General Assembly deliberation. As the introductory sentence says, "We, the member congregations of the Unitarian Universalist Association, covenant to affirm and promote" these Principles and Purposes—*covenant* being the key word. How this came about is told in detail by Edward A. Frost in his introductory chapter to *With Purpose and Principle*, a collection of essays he edited. Each chapter is by one of Frost's ministerial colleagues and deals with one of the seven Principles.

WOMEN WERE THE CATALYSTS

Much of the credit for initiating the long and meandering path that led to the final agreement must go to the women in our movement. For some years, women (although not women alone) had grown unhappy with the blatantly sexist language of the original Principles, and during the 1970s repeated "man hunts" were staged to remove the most offensive terminology from the bylaws. Excised, for instance, were the consistent references to the moderator and president, indeed to all officers and ministers, as "he." Even so, mentions of "brotherhood" and "mankind" survived well into the 1980s.

This, of course, was the time when the women's movement was gathering momentum nationally. NOW, the National Organization of Women, had been founded in 1966, and Unitarian Universalists—as is so often the case—were in the vanguard of those responding to the call for equity and recognition. Two other emerging sensibilities coalesced to make the existing Principles seem inadequate: first, the awareness that traditions other than Judeo-Christian are important to our heritage; second, that our relation to the environment is one of our primary religious concerns. The main impetus for change, however, came from the women in the denomination as they made their fellow Unitarian Universalists painfully aware that this critical part of our bylaws had blandly accepted social standards that for far too long had demeaned and denigrated women.

Natalie Gulbrandsen, who later served eight years as UUA moderator, joined the UUWF Board in 1971 and became president in 1978. Having been one of those who stayed up until 2:00 a.m. when the original Principles were hammered out, listening to "a lot of contentious speeches" and watching people get terribly upset, she had some idea of how heated General Assembly debates could get. She wasn't sure what to expect, therefore, when in 1977 the Joseph Priestley District, together with some women at the First Parish in Lexington, Massachusetts, put forward a Women and Religion resolution. Among its provisions the resolution called on leaders at all levels of the UUA to "make every effort to (a) put traditional assumptions and language in perspective, and (b) to avoid sexist assumptions and language in the future."

As it turned out, things went relatively smoothly. While some delegates couldn't accept that they or their association were patriarchal, "We explained it," Gulbrandsen recalls, "and it went through"—unanimously.

It helped that the UUWF members had done their homework, completing a survey of the number of women in the UU ministry (mighty few) and in positions of power (not anywhere near half), demonstrating rampant if perhaps unconscious sexism. According to Gulbrandsen, "We had all the facts and figures and convinced people that they didn't want that kind of reputation."

Two years later a Continental Conference on Women and Religion was held in Loveland, Ohio. One workshop was called "The UUA Principles: Do They Affirm Us as Women?" According to Edward Frost, the response from the participants was a resounding "*No!*" The delegates felt that the original UUA Principles not only failed to affirm them as women, "but they fail to indicate a respect for the wholeness of life and for the earth."

But even in her own church the need to adopt new Principles and Purposes was not universally accepted, Gulbrandsen remembers. She had to explain to the men in her church why references to "mankind" made women feel left out. "They said, 'Mankind' doesn't leave you out,'" she recalls. "I replied that we are human beings but not men, and that there are many other terms you could use—humankind, human beings—that include women." Nor did disagreement come only from men, Gulbrandsen says. "When we took the Women and Religion resolution to the IARF (the International Association for Religious Freedom), the English women were furious. Why would we want to do such a thing? they wanted to know. But we felt that a wave was coming in our direction and eventually we would prevail."

THE COMING WAVE

It was highly perceptive of UUA President Pickett to sense the coming of this wave. In Tom Owen-Towle's biography of Pickett, he is quoted as telling the Women and Religion Convocation, "You are changing the situation of women within our denomination and, in so doing, you are opening up for all of us new ways of understanding and perceiving women and, we hope, men as well. . . . By changing women's situation within the institution, your impact can be enormous in affecting sexist attitudes, assumptions, and behavior. Let us resolve to make it so." His welcoming the change was particularly surprising since, he had to admit, when one of his daughters had told him she was considering the Unitarian Universalist ministry he was taken by surprise. If he had had a son, he confessed, his entering the ministry would not have been unexpected, but it had never occurred to him that a daughter might decide to be a minister.

In 1981, a "desexed" and non-theistic revision of the original Principles drafted by various women's groups was presented to the General Assembly. It caused great uneasiness, especially among UU Christians, who saw it as tantamount to writing them out of the UUA, and a group of ministers circulated a letter expressing concern about the lack of any reference to our Christian roots and the dropping of any mention of God. As the letter said, "The impending debate on whether or not to amend [the Principles] so as to eliminate the word 'God' has every prospect of becoming the kind of contest in which, regardless of who wins, our Association will lose. . . . We believe that it is time to recognize and empower that pluralism which we are." It then called for open dialogue and the appointment of a committee to study the situation.

Denise (Denny) Davidoff, who had succeeded Gulbrandsen as UUWF president and was later to succeed her as moderator, made a bold decision. Even though it caused a serious rift among the women delegates, she broke with those who favored immediate adoption of the proposed draft. Persuaded that an immediate vote would be needlessly divisive, and in any case would probably lose, Davidoff endorsed the proposal that a committee be set up to study the issue and report back in a subsequent year. It was a far-sighted concession that not only avoided confrontation but led to the formulation of a far more eloquent and inclusive statement. It fulfilled the wish voiced by George "Kim" Beach, who along with Carl Scovel of Boston's King's Chapel was one of the ministers who had signed the letter of protest, for a statement "with religious integrity, intellectual coherence, and literary quality."

The motion to set up the committee passed, and it launched what Davidoff has described as "an enormously well-done, grass roots process."

Walter Royal Jones, Jr., a parish minister since retired who headed the special committee for much of its existence, recalls that they sent out questionnaires asking both congregations and individuals to submit suggestions. While some respondents expressed skepticism, considering the whole process a waste of time, the committee also received many contributions of great merit which, in turn, it circulated for comment. What happened then was what Jones describes as "the good old process" of posting big sheets of paper all over the meeting room walls. "There were seven members of the committee, and we had seven authors! We really wanted to assure everyone that no point of view was going to be left out. We wanted to say to everyone, *You belong.*"

Davidoff believes that it was this careful search for consensus that explains why the draft the committee eventually produced was adopted with relatively few changes and virtually no animosity.

A HEALING SOLUTION

But the continent-wide consultations took time. The Committee's first report was submitted at the New Brunswick, Maine, GA in 1982. "We met on the Bowdoin College campus," Davidoff recalls, "and broke into small groups to discuss the proposal. John Cummins [the first committee chair who was replaced by Jones almost immediately] had asked the Women's Federation to recruit one hundred discussion leaders, and I remember a beautiful day, sitting on the lawn to discuss the language."

According to Jones, it was committee member Harry Hoehler who came up with a solution to the problem that had created controversy both at the 1960 meeting and again in 1981: whether to make reference to the deity and the Judeo-Christian tradition. His suggestion was to divide the statement into two parts: seven Principles, followed by references to five "living traditions we share." (A sixth, referring to earth-centered traditions, was added in 1995.) Since the summaries of the traditions were in essence historical statements, no one objected to the inclusion of a reference to the "Jewish and Christian teachings which call us to respond to God's love." Jones rightly refers to this as a radical idea, which transformed a divisive issue into a formulation everyone could accept and that accurately reflected the diversity of UU views and beliefs.

After further revisions based on the 1982 discussions, the committee circulated a new draft to all congregations that was debated in 1983, and after some additional changes, a final draft was submitted to the General Assembly in 1984. After adopting an amendment to change the phrase "Respect for Earth and the interdependence of its living systems" to "Respect for the interdependent web of all existence of which we are a part," the delegates were ready for a final vote. "A resonant chorus said 'Aye,'" the *UU World* reported. "There was a scattering of 'No's.'" Added the reporter, stepping out of his role as an objective observer, "Suddenly, like a burst of sunlight after rain, the delegates realized what they had accomplished."

The final wording, Jones says, "had suddenly seemed to fall into place" at the committee's final session. The next year, as the bylaws require, this draft was again voted on at the Atlanta, Georgia, GA, where, again quoting the *World*, "More than a thousand voices roared, 'Aye.' A single male voice at the rear of the hall was heard to vote 'No.'" As Edward Frost describes the scene, there were "loud applause, sighs of relief, tears, and a few shrugs of 'wait and see.'"

REFLECTIONS FROM THE CHAIR

Writing in *First Days Record,* Walter Royal Jones has commented that while most of the wording of the new Principles and Purposes was different, most of the concepts had been anticipated in the 1961 statement ... with the exception of number seven: "Respect for the interdependent web of all existence of which we are a part." That principle, Jones explains, had not been anticipated, but "its inclusion was overwhelmingly mandated in the responses received from churches and fellowships, and its current happy wording emerged from the floor of the General Assembly, where it was instantly recognized as just the right language."

Another change Jones considers significant is the switch from "the free and disciplined search for truth" in the 1961 statement to "free and responsible search for truth and meaning," suggesting that the search take place in community. He also notes that the adjective *inherent* to qualify the worth of every person in place of *supreme* recognizes that the potentiality of every person is "capable of being hidden or rejected, even betrayed."

This, then, as amended in 1995, is the statement that has served us well for fifteen years.

We, the member congregations of the Unitarian Universalist Association, covenant to affirm and promote:

The inherent worth and dignity of every person;
Justice, equity, and compassion in human relations;
Acceptance of one another and encouragement to spiritual growth in our congregations;
A free and responsible search for truth and meaning;
The right of conscience and the use of the democratic process within our congregations and in society at large;
The goal of world community with peace, liberty, and justice for all;
Respect for the interdependent web of all existence of which we are a part.

The statement goes on to spell out the sources of the living tradition we share, concluding,

Grateful for the religious pluralism which enriches and enno-
bles our faith, we are inspired to deepen our understanding
and expand our vision. As free congregations we enter into this
covenant, promising to one another our mutual trust and
support.

"Apart from Quakers and their time-honored preference for
consensus," Jones reflects, "it is unlikely that the history of religion provides any comparable example of such intentional and
committed use of inclusive, non-hierarchical processes to produce a guiding statement. We are deeply indebted to the challenging insights of women's groups in our movement for this
aspect of the work."

FIFTEEN YEARS ON

Suggesting a theory as to why the "P&P" have served us so well
for fifteen years, Jones sums up:

> If we say to the world that these principles are sound, then
> there must be something true about our nature and our rela-
> tionship to the creative processes that operate in the universe,
> whether or not they are intentional. In all of the challenges,
> dilemmas, and ambiguities of life, ultimately we trust that you
> and I are alive. And that trust is implicit in the first principle:
> *the inherent worth and dignity of every person.* I know that
> Descartes is not in high favor in philosophical circles right now
> because of the emphasis he put on the supremacy of think-
> ing. But what he was really asking himself was: *is there any-
> thing I cannot really doubt?* And his answer was, if I am seeing
> this as a problem it proves that I am here. That is the
> inescapable reality, and I think the first principle captures
> some of that. There are all kinds of mysteries and speculations
> such as how we got here, but of the fact that we are here there
> can be no doubt.

But Jones is not suggesting that his committee produced a statement for the ages. After fifteen years, he feels, "we should not be
surprised at some restiveness. On the one hand, some are uneasy
with what they see as a kind of creeping creedalism in the way

we use them. On the other there is a perception of incompleteness, with important, arguably necessary empowering assumptions about cosmic reality and our particular place in it that 'P and P' leave unsaid." He also perceives dissatisfaction with overemphasis on the individual, so that "the creative nature of community and interdependence are only tardily and inadequately acknowledged."

Nonetheless, though no one at the moment is suggesting any drastic revisions, the fact remains that a statement committed to "a free and responsible search for truth and meaning" carries within it the seeds of its own obsolescence. Just consider: Well into the twentieth century, our Unitarian predecessors posted on their church walls a statement that in one of its various versions proclaimed that we believe in "The Fatherhood of God, the Brotherhood of Man, the Leadership of Jesus, Salvation through Character, and the Steady Progress of Mankind Onward and Upward Forever." Quite apart from the fact that we tend not to use so many capital letters, we would today have difficulty saying those words without embarrassment and lots of "sic-ness." Yet the people who did say them were just as intelligent, just as in tune with their times, just as committed to reason and free thinking as we are.

In 2020 (when everyone presumably will have perfect vision), our current Principles and Purposes may also be perceived to have inadequacies that require radical rewriting. And therein lies our genius. This process of change, rightly called renewal or regeneration, continues and, let us hope, will continue, for another twenty or even one hundred years.

SINGING THE LIVING TRADITION

Arthur Foote, a distinguished minister at the time of consolidation, chaired the commission that produced a new hymnal for the new denomination—*Hymns for the Celebration of Life*—in 1964. Mark Belletini, now the minister in Columbus, Ohio, who had been teaching liturgy at Starr King School, was asked to chair the commission that developed its successor, *Singing the Living Tradition*. He recalls,

When we were about halfway through the project, I went to visit Foote. He had retired by then to a small coastal village in Maine, and after some small talk he looked me in the eye and said, 'So how much of our work have you kept?' I was deeply moved by the question and said, 'Over half of it. Our commission sang through every hymn in the blue [1964] book three times, and it's an extraordinary book. We think you did a wonderful job.'

He told me stories about the people on his committee and how they had gone back to the red book that preceded their blue book, and I was deeply touched to hear the history of this living tradition. I told him which hymns we had kept and showed him sheets of the new hymns we were considering, including some spirituals and music from other traditions, and some we had commissioned. He looked at them on his lap and said, 'Young man, I can't read these any more. Will you sing them for me?' I knelt down next to his wooden-backed chair and sang the hymns and he wept and I wept. There was a sense of the living tradition at that moment that you only experience sometimes in a transcendent moment during the Service of the Living Tradition.

Their tears have nourished us all. To quote one of the hymns in the new book, "We laugh, we cry, we live, we die; we dance, we sing our song. We need to feel there's something here to which we can belong." And that is what both collections have done for us—made us feel there's something to which we can belong.

A SINGING FAITH

The 1964 volume was published "in the conviction," as the preface says, "that a vital faith must be a singing faith and that each generation needs to express itself freshly in its own idiom." From diverse times and cultures, the book brought together texts and music that seemed to the commission members to have timely meaning for the new denomination. It made wide use of classic hymn tunes as well as folk music from many lands, and included such traditional Protestant songs as Luther's "A Mighty

Fortress Is Our God," as well as many nineteenth-century Unitarian favorites, including three by James Russell Lowell, fifteen by Samuel Longfellow, and an astonishing eighteen by Frederick Lucian Hosmer. However, Longfellow was almost tied by Kenneth Patton with thirteen attributed hymns and readings, plus others labeled "anonymous" since Patton—a contemporary and fairly controversial Universalist preacher and poet—was himself a member of the hymnbook commission and even he, though far from a shrinking violet, thought that more might be considered excessive.

By the 1980s, many of the hymn texts were no longer acceptable. Hosmer's "Thy Kingdom Come, O Lord" offended on both theological and sexist grounds, while Lowell's great abolitionist hymn ("Men, whose boast it is that ye come of fathers brave and free, if there breathe on earth a slave, are ye truly free and brave?") not only left out women but used archaic language that today's worshippers are apt to stumble over. What was needed, it was widely felt, was a new hymnal to proclaim our theological diversity and celebrate the wider world in which we live.

This was the assignment given a new Hymnbook Resources Commission, appointed by the UUA board in 1987. Taking the new Principles and Purposes as the touchstones of the new collection, the commission labored for six years to complete its mission.

Selecting the readings was relatively easy; choosing the hymns was the tough part. Here is how Belletini recalls the work of the commission. The members (whose names are listed in front of the book) were "some of the finest people on earth, and we had a great six years. We broadcast an invitation to submit suggestions, and we lined up congregations that agreed to test new things to see whether they would fly. We initially met five times, then four times, a year, and we would sing until our throats were raw. There were no names of either composer or author on any of the stuff we reviewed, and if even one of the eight of us saw any merit in any of the hymns we would keep it to sing again. Sometimes we liked the tune but not the text; other times we felt the text was worthwhile but it needed another tune. And sometimes we found that people didn't understand the need for inclusive language."

The Commission sought to include material that would reflect the denomination's growing multicultural and ecological awareness, its greater acceptance of spiritual imagery, and above all its commitment to the inclusion of feminine imagery of the divine. Still more difficult was deciding what to do with the old favorites that were being sung Sunday after Sunday by congregations all over the continent, but whose texts offended some current sensibilities. Some were dropped altogether, and of the half that were kept a number were revised. The Lowell hymn was changed to: "All whose boast it is that we," and all national hymns disappeared. Gone, for instance, was "America the Beautiful," and for Canadians, no more "God Save the King (or Queen)." New were "Daya kar daan bhakti ka," a Hindu prayer for harmony and peace, and "Heleluyan," a traditional Muskogee Indian song.

The changes are reflected most clearly by a comparison of the two topical indexes of hymns, though that doesn't mean that all the hymns listed under the old headings were deleted. New headings include ecology, flower communion, gay and lesbian pride day, Islam, Kwanzaa, and pagan. Among the missing are Jesus, man, Whitsunday. Also worthy of note is that fully a third of the book is the work of Canadian and U.S. Unitarians, Universalists, and Unitarian Universalists, past and present. Reflecting UU roots and global awareness, there are works from England, Transylvania, Nigeria, the Philippines, India, and the Czech Republic.

A UUA staff member went about the tedious task of clearing copyrights and permissions. It wasn't always easy. The Commission badly wanted to include John Lennon's "Imagine," but couldn't get permission to change his phrase, "the brotherhood of man." Similarly, folk singer Pete Seeger, though himself a UU, said they could use his songs the way he wrote them or not at all, so for the sake of inclusive language he, too, got left out.

Because the Commission members were not well known, there was some distrust of whether they would go too far in throwing out old hymns, so they made special efforts to report on their progress. "We worked our butts off at General Assemblies," Belletini says, "teaching new hymns, leading rounds and chants, leading worship. We had discussions with people, and found that there was a great deal of fear and a great deal of joy mixed together."

Obviously (at least if you know Unitarian Universalists), not everyone has been happy with the new hymnal. One minister, John Corrado, wrote in *First Days Record,* "The grab bag selection from various religions, 'Goddess,' 'solstice and equinox,' 'pagan,' certainly indicates a high degree of willingness to be undiscerningly eclectic. Why doesn't this respect for everybody and everything extend to dearly loved Christmas carols?" (Says Belletini: "Why use words on December 25 that we wouldn't find acceptable on the twenty-sixth?") Corrado also asks: "Why do we have a 'Hiroshima Day' but not 'Pearl Harbor Day'?" among the readings. (Belletini recalls that it was Mennonite friends who first pointed out to him that nationalistic hymns have no place in a religious book.) But then, as Corrado also points out, some useful stuff that was included in the 1935 *Beacon Song and Service Book* didn't make it into the 1964 *Hymns for the Celebration of Life.* Perhaps, someday, we can have an on-line hymnal that is all-inclusive and still not too heavy to lift—sort of a Psalm Pilot.

In any case, Belletini says, a typical UU congregation routinely uses only some 30 hymns, concluding, "There are 415 hymns in this book. If you can't find at least 30 you like, you're just too fussy to live."

Arthur Foote told Belletini that the years he spent on the hymnbook commission were the high point of his life. Belletini still has many years left, but he thinks that when his whole life story is told he will say the same thing. The rest of us can bask in the glow of the enthusiasm, devotion, and creativeness of all the members of both commissions. They have served us well.

SHARING THE MESSAGE

May all who come within our reach be kindled by our inner glow.

John Andrew Storey, no. 307

We now had words, symbols, and songs that we cherish in common, giving us a strong sense of self-identity and making us, as Carl Scovel has pointed out in an article in *UU Voice*, a classic denomination. That, he goes on to say, holds us together but can also limit our growth and outreach. The challenge ever since consolidation has been to have it both ways: to enjoy the benefits of community (so that through common effort we may better understand and shape the meaning of our lives), while also doing our best to grow (so that we may be more effective in building a just and peaceful world). One way to achieve both objectives is to find better ways of keeping in touch with one another.

This was the rationale behind one of Robert West's primary campaign promises when he ran for the UUA presidency—to start a denominational newspaper that would be mailed free of charge to every member family. It was a pledge he promptly kept, and as soon as he took office every congregation was asked to supply the names and addresses of its members. In March of

1970, an eight-page tabloid called *Unitarian Universalist World* was launched, aimed at providing timely, two-way communications not only between headquarters and the entire UU membership, but among local congregations, districts, and denominational organizations. At first, the paper was published nineteen times a year, reaching approximately one hundred thousand households. It replaced the denominational magazine, *UUA Now,* a successor to the *Register-Leader* which, in turn, carried on the tradition of the *Unitarian* (originally *Christian*) *Register* and the *Universalist* (originally *Christian*) *Leader.* The magazine had been available only by subscription and hence reached only a relatively small number of readers.

The *Unitarian Universalist World* brought members of every UU congregation word of board actions, news of what was happening in the districts, significant events in local churches and fellowships, and coverage of General Assemblies. Thus, it was hoped, it would not only provide a link that would make all Unitarian Universalists feel connected with the larger denominational family, but also give headquarters staff a better way of keeping up with what was happening in the member societies.

In 1987, the *World,* as it was then renamed, was turned back into a magazine, in the hope, as President Schulz explained the change, that it would reach a broader, non-UU audience. This was a time when personal journalism reached its crest, as Tom Wolfe and his imitators turned the reportorial eye into the reportorial "I." The *World* followed this pattern, turning for a while into a journal of reflection and opinion. Later editors again revised this format, emphasizing feature articles about people, trends, and events with a denominational tie-in, plus news columns about both continental and local developments.

Today, renamed *UU World,* the magazine is putting still greater emphasis on stories directly related to the denomination, with features recalling our history, relevant religious news items from other sources, as well as essays, readings, and meditations with a UU orientation. As Editor-in-Chief Thomas Stites has explained, "This [latest name change] should end the confusion with the eight other magazines named the *World,* including one published by conservative Christians in Virginia. [It] also better reflects the magazine's mission."

The UUA also publishes a newsletter called *InterConnections* that once a quarter provides an exchange of practical hints and information for leaders and professional staff of local congregations. It is also available to everyone else on-line.

THE E-DENOMINATION

That, of course, is not the only way electronic communication has enhanced our ability to stay in touch with UUA headquarters and with each other, and thus to enhance our sense of a common identity.

In the pre-electronic age, one of the weaknesses of the UUA was the sense of isolation felt by many of the member congregations. Even if they actively participated in their district or cluster group activities, it was usually only a small percentage of the members who ever met any Unitarian Universalists from a church or fellowship other than their own. This was especially true of people not in major population centers, where the nearest sister congregation might be several hours' drive away. Online communication—while not quite as personal as a face-to-face encounter—has changed that, putting both individuals and congregations in easy touch with each other: with their districts, with affinity groups, and with continental headquarters.

The UUA's office of electronic communications estimates that at least 65 percent of adult Unitarian Universalists have online capabilities, and the number increases month by month. Also:

- More than 70 percent of member congregations now have websites linked to that of the UUA.
- The number of "hits" to the UUA web page is growing dramatically, now averaging forty-one thousand a month and going up by some 30 percent a year.
- On any given Sunday, more than 150 people will find out about a UU congregation they can visit by checking www.uua.org on the web.

- In the three years since the debut of the completed UUA website it has generated more than one million "hits," quickly approaching 1.5 million.
- There are more than 170 electronic (e-mail) mailing lists that can be used to reach Unitarian Universalists with common interests—fellow ministers, religious educators, board presidents, youth leaders, choir directors, new members—whoever might be able to help with a professional or volunteer responsibility or just engage in a mutually enjoyable conversation.
- Numerous UU chat rooms keep springing up, stimulating electronic networking to exchange information and ideas, or to engage in discussion and debate.

In addition, the UUA website provides access to committee reports, GA resolutions, and other actions, both current and archival, many entries going back to consolidation in 1961. It also provides links to related organizations, such as the UU Service Committee, the UU Ministers Association, the Young Adult Caucus, as well as to more informal common interest groups such as newsletter editors, parents, ministers serving large churches, and the more unexpected groups, such as Unitarian Universalists in Finland. For entertainment, you can even click on "UU Humor."

Meanwhile, the Electronic Communications Committee is exploring ways to let people participate in General Assembly deliberations in real time and, possibly, even to vote.

Nor is that the only way in which the Internet is being put to use. It also enables the association to improve communications with the media. For example, the very day the news broke that the Supreme Court had ruled that the Boy Scouts could exclude gays, the UUA home page offered a statement by President John Buehrens deploring the decision and offering background on the UUA's position on the issue. Thus we can talk not only to each other but also to the wider world in ways more timely, more efficient, and less expensive than ever before possible.

Thomas Jefferson famously said that due to the lack of a nearby church he had to be content to be a Unitarian by himself. While membership in an active congregation is still the ideal way to be a UU, the Internet has at least provided a second-best alternative. Just as important, it can put those who *are* active members in touch with each other regardless of where they live, and it has also vastly expanded the potential of the Church of the Larger Fellowship.

THE CHURCH OF THE LARGER FELLOWSHIP

The Church of the Larger Fellowship (CLF) is our "non-resident" congregation. It has its own minister and religious education director, who serve twenty-seven hundred members in North America and overseas. Founded in 1944 as an extension effort of the AUA, it is now an independent congregation serving not only isolated Unitarian Universalists, but people who are not mobile, such as hospitalized patients or prisoners, and those who for personal reasons do not feel comfortable in their nearest congregation. Some members hold dual membership—and pledge —in another congregation; others are ministers who don't have their own church. In addition, CLF supports tiny congregations with its "church on loan" program, making worship resources available to groups that gather on Sunday mornings but aren't of a size sufficient to develop their own worship and religious education (RE) materials.

Once a month, every CLF member family receives *Quest,* providing eight pages of sermons, news, meditations and prayers, together with messages from the minister and RE director. Prominently displayed are the minister's 800 number and e-mail address, so that members can contact her for answers to questions, religious dialogue, crisis counseling, professional referrals, or other types of pastoral support.

The minister, Jane Rzepka, stresses how electronic communication has enhanced her ability to maintain personal, if long-distance, relationships with her congregation. "We have made great strides with our website," she says. "In addition to all the general information and resources we offer, it's now possible to become a member, pledge, gain access to our library catalogue, or to read *Quest* on-line. In fact, 90 percent of our inquiries now come by e-mail, though we still get—and answer—handwritten letters."

In addition, members from all over the world can communicate with one another on three e-mail lists—including one devoted to religious education—while a chat room makes it possible for members to link up on Sunday mornings to exchange "joys and concerns" and other personal interaction. "Some sit at home," says Rzepka," playing some music, even lighting a candle." To further enhance their religious experience, they can borrow books, audio- and videotapes, or a set of worship materials called "A Month of Sundays," which includes four complete services, as well as children's stories.

CLF members with children are also provided with a parent handbook, loans of UUA curricula, and regular mailings of *Connections,* a periodical for parents, and either *uu&me* for seven to twelve year-olds, or *Synapse* for teens. There is also ready access to Betsy Hill Williams, the RE director, who says that her goal is "to help parents and children meet the challenges of family life today with greater intention and spiritual awareness."

A good index of the importance of CLF in our denominational life is that after Eugene Pickett left the UUA presidency he chose to serve as its minister. An even better index is the mail reaching Rzepka from the members:

· "At one time in my life I didn't live near a UU congregation. The CLF was my lifeline."
· "The congregation I attend has veered away from mainstream Unitarian Universalism. I belong for the community, but I need a regular dose of solid UUism—something with substance!"
· "I'm a minister, and I appreciate belonging to a church of my own."

Others write that they found the CLF website, got a taste of Unitarian Universalism from a safe distance without family or neighbors knowing, and finally moved into a "bricks-and-mortar" congregation. But with clicks and bytes rather than bricks and mortar, the Church of the Larger Fellowship is one of our most vibrant congregations.

VOICES FOR GOOD

The denomination's tradition of progressive religious publishing goes back to the mid-1800s with the American Unitarian Association and the New England Universalist Publishing House. It is a tradition reinforced but certainly not replaced by the electronic media, and today there are two UUA publishing ventures: Skinner House Books and Beacon Press.

Named after Clarence Skinner, a Universalist writer, teacher, and minister who served as dean of the School of Religion at Tufts University from 1933 to 1945, it is the mission of Skinner House Books to publish titles related to Unitarian Universalist faith, history, and beliefs. The imprint publishes in a variety of genres, including meditation manuals, church resources, spiritual memoirs, histories, and biographies. The 2000-2001 Skinner House catalog includes such liberal classics as Conrad Wright's book on congregational polity and James Luther Adams's *On Being Human Religiously;* others are brand new, such as Joseph Fabry's memoir, *Making Sense,* which he completed just before he died in 1999, or *Thoreau as a Spiritual Guide* by Barry M. Andrews. The UUA website provides quick access to the Skinner House Book and Beacon Press catalogs.

Beacon Press publishes books that have a reach far beyond our denominational boundaries, speaking not just to our own members but disseminating our message to the larger world. Since that was the purpose for which the American Unitarian Association was founded, it is in a sense our longest continuous denominational activity. As an 1821 *Christian Register* editorial observed, "the importance of the book is to be estimated by the number of minds upon which it may be made to operate." Today, Beacon Press carries on that mission, taking as its identifying slogan that it is "Unitarian Universalism's voice for good in the world."

During AUA days, Beacon published a collection of the anti-McCarthy cartoons by "Herblock" (Herbert Block) of the *Wash-*

ington Post, as well as Paul Blanshard's highly controversial *American Freedom and Catholic Power*—so controversial, in fact, that not only would no other publisher touch it but the *New York Times* refused even to accept advertising. Beacon also accepted—all other publishers having turned it down—Victor Frankl's *Man's Search for Meaning,* which went on to sell well over three million copies and made the Nazi concentration camp experience come alive for millions of readers. The point is not only that such books make constructive impacts on public policy and thinking, but that were it not for Beacon Press, many would never appear at all. Earl Grollman, a retired rabbi whose books on coping with death have become best sellers, told the *UU World* that he took his proposal to Beacon because it "was the pioneer in working with problems that nobody else would handle."

It is impossible to estimate the number of minds Beacon Press books have influenced over the years, but worthwhile as the effort has been, the cost has often stretched the resources of the denomination, typified by the deficit run up by publication of the Pentagon Papers. But that wasn't the last time the press ran in the red, and by the late 1970s things were so bad that President Carnes pushed for selling the press to a private investor. On top of the money problems, the press seemed to lose its sense of direction, publishing fiction and poetry that neither spoke for UU values nor covered their cost. The UUA Board agreed with Carnes that it was time to sell the press.

Under the leadership of Jeanette Hopkins, a publishing professional and former senior editor at Beacon, a small group determined to stop the sale. Hopkins recalls pleading with the UUA Board: "I made a very eloquent statement, asking who would publish the anti-McCarthy books if another such period of repression were to come about, but it made no impression whatever."

She then formed a committee that recruited two congregations —deliberately choosing one that had been actively pro-BAC and the other pro-BAWA to show there was unity on this issue—and obtained a temporary injunction to forbid the sale, whereupon the Board agreed to submit the decision to the General Assembly.

The GA agenda had already been printed, but Hopkins and her supporters posted notices wherever they could and slipped them under delegates' hotel room doors, inviting people to come to a meeting to air the issue. When Sandra Caron, the moderator, gave three of the group's leaders time to address the plenary session, they pleaded that if the board insisted on selling the press, it at least be sold not to a private investor but to a non-profit corporation they had begun to set up which was pledged to preserve Beacon's UU identity. The reaction of the GA delegates persuaded the board to rescind its decision.

THE BEACON SHINES AGAIN

By 1983, when Wendy Strothman was named Beacon's new director, the financial situation was still pretty shaky and the press had yet to rediscover its editorial mission. Under Strothman's direction, it overcame both ailments; indeed it enjoyed some of its best, most successful years. "We set out," she explains, "to raise the editorial standards and to publish a more focused collection of books. We also concentrated on quality, deciding not to publish any books unless they were really the best works on the subject we could find."

It took three years, but gradually Beacon moved into the black and once again became a bold voice for UU principles. Concentrating on women's studies, it scored a critical and commercial triumph in 1992 by publishing Marian Wright Edelman's *The Measure of Our Success,* which became a bestseller and was included in that year's *New York Times* list of notable books.

"We also revived the back list," Strothman adds. "There were some gems on Beacon's list that had been allowed to languish. In addition, we went out and commissioned books by noteworthy authors rather than wait for things to land on our desk. That's how we got Marian's book, and also Cornel West's *Race Matters*"— another best seller that spoke forcefully on a critical national problem. Furthermore, Beacon set up an advisory board of publishing executives and scholars to help guide its policies.

It was also Strothman who, to make sure all Beacon books reflected the denomination's objectives, required that her editors put on every editorial proposal a comment on how the book supported the UUA's Principles and Purposes. She did not think, however, it was a wise strategy to promote Beacon as a denominational press. "It's very important for Beacon not to be seen as an organ of the UUA," she explains. "Beacon provides good service by being a public voice that promotes our religious values, but if it were seen as a religious organ, its books wouldn't get reviewed in any major newspaper."

A CONTINUING MISSION

Today, according to Helene Atwan, the current director, Beacon is "still striving to reflect the Principles and Purposes of the UUA in all of their complexity . . . to bring the mission of the UUA into the broader world."

Among today's topics of concentration are religion, women's issues, gay and lesbian concerns, economics, race, and class. Also, Beacon recently published two novels by Gayle Jones, an African American writer who, through fiction, confronts the issues of race and cultural identity. "We were, I think, the first trade press to publish on transgender people," Atwan adds, "and, of course, we continue to publish on burning political issues. In fact, anytime we mention Beacon Press to outsiders you'd be surprised how often they say, 'Oh yes, the Pentagon Papers.'"

She points out that the political books are not about issues "that only last about twenty minutes," but about basic concerns relating to the political process and how people can take a meaningful part in it. A recent example is *All Souls*, Michael McDonald's story about growing up poor in an Irish section of South Boston and learning to be an activist. Other recent noteworthy Beacon publications include Geoffrey Canada's *Reaching Up For Manhood: Transforming the Lives of Boys in America*, and Ronald V. Dellums's *Lying Down with the Lions*, in which he chronicles his rise to the House of Representatives and his commitment to democratic social change.

Then, of course, there are also works of inspiration, such as New York City UU minister Forrest Church's *Lifecraft,* and a new edition of Thoreau's *Walden.*

Financially, 2000 turned out to be a good year, but deficits in the two previous years led the UUA Board to name a task force on strategic options headed by Robert Lavender, a former financial advisor and UUA board member. They are exploring ways of assuring the long-term stability that is essential if Beacon is to prevail as a counterpoise to right-wing foundations that initiate, subsidize, and promote such books as *The Bell Curve* and *America in Black and White.* Given the resources of these foundations it is a somewhat uneven struggle, but Atwan hopes that electronic publishing, by reducing production costs and switching backlist volumes that the press can no longer afford to warehouse to "print-on-demand" distribution, may make it possible to greatly increase the reach of Beacon books. On-line bookstores may also help, though the rapid disappearance of independent retailers is hurtful.

Despite its Perils-of-Pauline financial life, Beacon Press has been a tremendous boon not only to the denomination but to society. As Atwan points out, today's publishing environment makes it harder and harder for books that are not expected to be money makers to find a publisher. "The commercial presses just don't want to do serious books. By publishing such books," she concludes, "Beacon is uniquely qualified to add to the public discussion. It is our mission to change people's minds—and lives."

A MORE VISIBLE PRESENCE

Conveying our ideas and ideals to the larger world is critical for wider acceptance of our principles, but it presupposes a healthy institution. Ensuring the institution's health in turn requires that we enlist at least some of those who share our convictions in joining our common enterprise. Yet we have often been skittish, to say the least, about engaging in anything that might be construed as evangelism.

Sometimes our diffidence goes too far: many of the churches built in the decades after World War II are situated in pretty garden spots, hard to find and invisible from major roadways. On the other hand, we also realize that if there were as many Unitarian Universalists as there are, say, Southern Baptists, we would get equal attention from the media and politicians. On the local level, there is a critical mass that's essential to be able to provide the variety of programs necessary to meet all the members' needs, to be an effective voice for justice in the community, and to pay the bills necessary for survival.

As Scott Alexander says in *Salted with Fire*, the book he edited about UU strategies for sharing faith and growing congregations, "As the radical religious right has unashamedly attempted to influence both public policy and private morality . . . , religious liberals have slowly awakened to the fact that we remain silent and hidden about what *we* believe and dream at our own peril." If we continue to remain silent, he goes on, "then by default it will be the beliefs and dreams of *others* that will influence and instruct the shape of our society and the lives of those around us."

For too long we did remain silent and were, in fact, slow to grow despite admonitions on the part of our leaders not to be selfish about hugging our insights too tightly to our chest. Said John Murray, "Give the people something of your new vision. . . . Give them not hell but hope and courage, preach the kindness and everlasting love of God." More recently, UUA President John Buehrens expressed the same thought this way: "I believe that the world needs our faith, now perhaps more than it ever has. I also believe that we are called to be a stronger, more visible presence of hope and healing."

After the shooting at the Columbine high school in Littleton, Colorado, Joel Miller, minister of the Columbine UU Church, paid moving tribute to what "hope and healing" can mean when tragedy strikes. In a letter to Friends of the UUA, he described how he rushed from his office when he first learned of the gunfire at the school. The police directed him to the place where the terrified students and their worried parents had gathered. "For the first hour I was the only clergy there," he reports. "Throughout the following days, there was an outpouring of support from Unitarian Universalists around the country." He goes on, "We were able to be there for the people who needed us because we received the support needed to establish the Columbine church," citing the UUA training program for the founding leaders, and the fact that the first minister had been called through the denomination's New Congregation Ministry Program.

NUMBERS MATTER (AND NUMBER MATTERS)

The New Congregation Ministry program is only one aspect of our renewed interest in outreach, and it is starting to show results.

In 2000, President John Buehrens was able to report to the General Assembly that there were five times as many UU high school youths as in 1992, and six times as many UU college groups, and Larry Ladd reported that adult membership had grown 11 percent since 1985, with religious education enrollment up 57 percent. "This is a wonderful time to be the financial advisor of the Association," Ladd commented. "There is energy and excitement throughout our growing movement. As a result, membership and revenues are growing." The 2000 GA itself serves as an index of expansion: there were 2,173 delegates representing 612 congregations in Nashville, Tennessee, with a total registration of 3,429 adults and 418 youth, setting an all-time record. By way of comparison, in 1984, the number of delegates in Columbus, Ohio, was 1,258, with a total attendance of only 1,800.

People with long memories may feel that these membership figures, while they show encouraging recent growth, are not much better than those at the time of consolidation, and it's true that in 1961 there were roughly 1,000 member congregations, representing a reported total of slightly more than 150,000 adults. What's more, Dana Greeley hoped that we could double our numbers in ten years, and in 1968, when membership peaked at 177,000, the UUA Goals Committee reported to the

Denver General Assembly that by 1980 we might well have 1,500 societies and 500,000 members. Instead, by the end of the twentieth century we were back at around 1,000 congregations and a total membership of only slightly more than 150,000 adults.

How to put these apparent contradictions in perspective? First of all, the 1961 numbers are suspect. Unlike current figures, they lump together adult membership and RE enrollment. Also, there was a notable shift in the number of members reported by the congregations once their "fair share" contributions to the Annual Program Fund were based on membership: suddenly pocketbook protection replaced euphoria as the main reporting criterion. And, finally, the immediate post-World War II years were a time when all denominations were growing; then they lost members in the late 1960s and 1970s, and while we began to recover in the 1980s, the mainline Protestant groups have continued to shrink. As for the number of member societies, consolidation could not save the smaller, often weak and rural Universalist churches. Ladd looked up the Universalist churches listed in the 1961 UUA directory and then checked how many of them were still there in 1999. "You can count the number that have survived on your fingers and toes," he found. Similarly, many of the Unitarian fellowships that were founded in the 1940s and 1950s—some with as few as ten members— usually were lay-led and at times so strongly anti-clerical that they refused to call a minister even when they grew. Not surprisingly, many faded away as the founders' generation disappeared.

All that may sound too much like alibis, and while some of the apparent decline was indeed the result of different standards of reporting, some of it was real. The dissension of the late 1960s undoubtedly led to a loss of morale. In a chapter in Alexander's book, John Morgan recalls a study he conducted for the Department of Extension of 315 congregations that had died between 1961 and 1983. Morgan, who has served as an extension minister in small congregations that were seeking to grow, again and again found among those that faltered "a familiar refrain: inwardness, focusing on internal questions while neglecting a wider mission." But if financial support of an institution by its members is a valid thermometer of underlying health, the recovery that began in the 1980s is continuing to improve.

MONEY AND MORALE

When President Pickett launched a capital campaign called Visions for Growth in 1983, it succeeded in raising about $4 million. A further campaign, called Handing on the Future, was initiated in 1993 just as William Schulz was ending his term, and by 1997, when John Buehrens had succeeded him, it had added $13.65 million in commitments to the association's coffers. Now we have embarked on The Campaign for Unitarian Universalism, which has made a promising start towards its ambitious goal of raising at least $32 million, money that will be used for sharing our vision; for strengthening our programs for children, youth, and young adults; for helping our churches grow; and for providing financial aid to UU ministerial students.

Contributions to the operating budget show a similarly encouraging record. Since 1985, congregational support of the Annual Program Fund has doubled in terms of constant dollars, and not only have the number of Friends of the UUA risen by 62 percent but the average individual contribution has gone up by 72 percent. Ladd, in citing these figures, calls them "symbolic of extraordinary levels of stewardship and commitment by our congregations and their members."

The turnabout in morale is a tribute to UU leadership at all levels. Even in the discouraging days of the 1970s, Robert West launched a program called "Sharing in Growth," which sought to help congregations both to grow in numbers and to improve the quality of their programs by focusing on the warmth, breadth, depth, and growth of their religious life. However, when Eugene Pickett took over as president after the death of Paul Carnes, he considered the need to reverse what he perceived as a general malaise to be his greatest challenge. "There was a poor working relationship between the administration and the board," he recalls, "poor relations between the association and the theological schools . . . religious education needed revamping . . . Liberal Religious Youth had gone almost out of existence . . . and many of our programs were just holding their own."

Yet in a sense he felt he was taking over at a good time—"we were ready for something to happen"—and he resolutely set about tackling every one of the problems he had identified. The first order of business, he concluded, had to be improving relations with the board, which he did by cultivating personal relationships and "inundating them with information," to overcome the suspicion that the administration was holding out on them. His next priority was to fix the financial situation. Not only did he launch a capital campaign, he went all around the country to attend fund-raising dinners—even though he hated asking for money and was shy about public speaking. Even more significantly, he launched direct appeals for individual support under the banner of Friends of the UUA.

Among his other initiatives, Pickett appointed a commission on religious education to stimulate development of new curriculums, and worked on reviving a youth program. It was also during his term that the Veatch program underwrote the financial stability of the association with its $20-million grant, making possible such new outreach programs as the extension ministry, which provides congregations with financial assistance in retaining ministers who have been specially trained in congregational growth and development. Over the last ten years, according to William Sinkford, UUA director for congregational, district, and extension services, this program has helped more than one hundred small congregations achieve full-time ministry. It is no coincidence that before Pickett's term ended, membership figures were moving upward. "It was not a lot," Pickett himself says with typical modesty about his effort to stimulate growth, "but at least it initiated discussion and got people excited." It did more: it revived morale. Increasingly, people felt good about their denomination, became more willing to support their local congregations as well as the continental association, and became more willing to tell their friends about their faith.

It's ironic that despite all these achievements, Pickett never felt comfortable in the public role at which Dana Greeley had excelled. A highly complimentary biography of him by a younger fellow minister, Tom Owen-Towle, makes several references to his self-doubts and moments of depression. Asked whether he would have liked to run again, Pickett told Owen-Towle, "No, I think I wanted to quit while things were going well and I was feeling good," adding, "Now Dana said he would stay forever . . . but I wanted to make sure I got out intact."

As the good institutionalist he calls himself, Pickett has remained active on behalf of our movement. After completing his term as president and then becoming minister of the Church of the Larger Fellowship, he took on first the presidency of the International Association for Religious Freedom (IARF), and then the challenging job of chairing the Ministerial Fellowship Committee.

EASING THE GROWING PAINS

Expanding on the extension ministry program, the UUA now also helps new congregations with its "Rapid Start" model, in which it supports the work of both a parish minister and a professional religious educator. The rationale is that even with the help of an extension minister, new congregations often get stuck at about 150 members. At that level the members of the congregation begin to feel they no longer know everyone, the minister may see newcomers not as an opportunity but as another list of names and faces to remember, and in fact a larger congregation is often more than one person can handle. Having two professionals on board, according to Sinkford, helps congregations reach the critical mass needed for a vibrant RE program, for adult education classes, for special interest groups, and for all the other programs that make for continued growth.

Currently, the Department of Congregational, District, and Extension Services is experimenting with other new models for stimulating growth, especially in metropolitan centers, as well as continuing such standard growth strategies as workshops and conferences for congregations of different sizes, field staff support, and leadership training weekends. Altogether, the department is in what Sinkford describes as a "learning mode," trying to analyze what works best and where, and why some churches are flourishing while comparable ones are not. "All of our programs," he says, "help congregations claim growth as central to their mission and try to equip the ordained and lay leadership to achieve it."

When it comes to encouraging growth, however, nothing can beat the enthusiasm of individual members in talking to their friends, for as one of our favorite hymns puts it, "The human touch can light the flame."

THE LIVING TRADITION OF MINISTRY

Be that teacher faith directs.
Carl Seaburg, no. 124

In our tradition of congregational polity, each congregation calls its own minister and it is not unheard of for a church to ordain one of its own lay members. Almost universally, however, it is recognized that picking a minister without academic qualifications and some sort of certification can be almost as dangerous as handing an untrained person a scalpel and saying, "I want you to be my surgeon." Deciding to do together what they cannot do alone, the member congregations have therefore decided that the education and credentialing of a pool of trained and qualified ministers is one of the tasks to be delegated to the denomination—to our theological schools and the UUA, respectively. Between them, they maintain a tradition going back for many decades, long before there was a UUA.

A LEARNED MINISTRY

The emotional highlight for those fortunate enough to be able to attend a General Assembly comes on Sunday morning at the Service of the Living Tradition. With the help of a booming organ, hundreds of Unitarian Universalists from all parts of North America stand, as the clergy, bedecked in academic robes and colorful stoles, march in singing "Rank by rank again we stand." It is a moment when even the most ascetic and aseptic humanists are apt to catch their breath.

For fifty-five years this service has been our way of honoring ministers who have completed full-time service, of commemorating those who have died in the last twelve months, and of welcoming with joy and acclamation those who are just entering into fellowship. About half of these new ministers are graduates of one of our two denominational seminaries. Before consolidation, there were four such schools, with each of the founding denominations having affiliations with two. In addition, Harvard Divinity School—having been founded to provide the "learned ministry" the Puritan tradition required and then becoming the intellectual hotbed of nineteenth-century Unitarianism—had a long tradition of preparing Unitarian and Unitarian Universalist ministers. While many UU theological students still go to Harvard, the school is now determinedly non-denominational, and there is no longer a single Unitarian Universalist on the faculty. Other new ministers receiving fellowship are graduates of schools that are either non-denominational or affiliated with other denominations.

At the time of consolidation, both of the Universalist schools —St. Lawrence and Crane Theological School at Tufts—were closed, one for lack of students, the other for lack of funds. That left two denominational schools: Meadville/Lombard in Chicago and the Starr King School for the Ministry in Berkeley, California. It's important to point out that denominational does not mean that they are part of the UUA. They are both independent institutions, each with its own board of trustees, each with its academic affiliation—the University of Chicago in the case of Meadville/Lombard, and in the case of Starr King the Graduate Theological Union which, in turn, is affiliated with the University of California.

So what makes them part of the UU family?

Above all, the fact that they see themselves as Unitarian Universalist schools whose students mainly (though not exclusively) plan to go into the UU ministry, and that their faculties and even more so their boards are generally made up of Unitarian Universalists. But as in any family, the members don't always get along, and the point of friction is often money.

Shortly before consolidation, Dana Greeley recalls in *25 Beacon Street,* Starr King School applied to the denomination for a modest $11,000 for operating expenses. In addition to "trying to help with finance in an emergency situation," according to Greeley, the AUA set up a Committee to Study Theological Education, which retained Harold Taylor, former president of Sarah Lawrence College, to conduct the study. Soon after consolidation, the "Taylor Report" dropped a bombshell, recommending that the number of denominational schools be cut and that Meadville/Lombard and Starr King be given UUA support. The cuts happened but the funding did not, and it was also proposed that Starr King give up its degree programs, which concentrated on adult education, making Meadville/Lombard the denomination's sole theological school.

The recommendation was not accepted, and Starr King happily survived, with UUA support becoming somewhat more generous, though never entirely adequate. During the 1970s, the UUA board again felt the need to study what was happening at the two seminaries. The report it received from one of its members indicated that Meadville/Lombard was educating only a bare handful of students, while Starr King, with more students, was having trouble keeping its financial head above water.

What to do? Step one was once again to appoint a committee, which this time was headed by Carl Scovel, minister of King's Chapel. "There was a feeling that each school was running its own show and not preparing their students for the ministry," according to Scovel. "There was also a desire to articulate common standards for all students, including those not attending UU seminaries . . . that there should be some common expectation for all people coming before the Fellowship Committee."

To meet these needs, the Scovel committee developed a grid as to what should be expected of all students, putting strong emphasis on clinical pastoral education and proposing that all ministerial candidates serve a well-structured internship. The report also stressed the importance of providing continuing education programs for ministers. As might be expected, the committee's recommendation caused considerable controversy, the theological schools pointing out that the UUA was calling for additional expenditures without providing the funds. However, the Scovel report and the follow-up initiatives of West and Picket shaped the educational priorities and standards that are basic to our denomination today.

THE NEXT STEP

After completing their academic training, candidates for the UU ministry are expected to enter into a year of internship supervised by a UU parish minister. They are then qualified to be accepted into the fellowship of UU ministers or, in the jargon of the profession, to be "fellowshipped." To supervise this process, the UUA has created a Ministerial Fellowship Committee (MFC). This group of fourteen volunteers, half clergy, half lay people, appointed by the Board of Trustees, meets with every single person who wants to be accepted into the UU ministry. Working together with the Ministerial Education Office of the Department of Ministry, the Committee seeks to assure—by reviewing transcripts, checking references, and interviewing candidates—that every candidate meets certain basic requirements, academic, personal, and professional.

The granting of fellowship is a rigorous, two-step process. Step one is to extend preliminary fellowship to those the MFC considers qualified. After completing three years of successful ministry, candidates are considered for final fellowship. A recent change to the process addresses the complaint that meeting with the MFC only at the end of seminary is unnecessarily stressful. In response, the committee has set up six regional subcommittees that meet with the students during their years of schooling so as to give guidance as to what courses they might need to add and how to prepare for the final review. Such guidance in some cases involves the suggestion that they might reconsider their choice of career. While hearing such advice is tough, it beats having put in years of preparation only to face a "sudden death" decision at the end of the line. Says Diane Miller, head of the Department of Ministry, "There are very few such people, maybe three or four a year, and usually they've been told all along but just didn't hear it. But the real value of this new program is that it creates a welcoming, challenging atmosphere that helps shape strong ministerial leaders."

An additional change to the process has been the enlargement of the Fellowship Committee so that now two separate panels can, between them, interview more applicants than the prior single panel could handle on its own. At the same time, the number of applicants seems to have crested, possibly because the regional sub-committees of the MFC screen out some potential candidates earlier on.

In becoming a parish minister there is, of course, one major hurdle yet to come: finding a pulpit.

MATCHMAKING

The Settlement Office of the Department of Ministry is, in effect, the employment agency that brings ministers and congregations together.

When a congregation is looking to fill a ministry position, it elects a ministerial search committee, which then furnishes the Settlement Office with extensive information to be posted on the UUA website. Ministers looking for a position—whether they are first-timers or looking to make a change—look over the list and let the office know whether they have an interest in any of the open positions. The Settlement Office then forwards equally extensive information about the minister to the Committee.

"If both church and minister remain interested in pursuing a courtship," says John Weston, head of the office, "they exchange packets of information, followed by telephone interviews. The search committee then interviews the finalists in person and hears them preach at neutral locations." Generally it then recommends one of them to the congregation as its candidate. "The ministerial candidate spends a week with the congregation, preaching on two Sundays, meeting board members and parishioners . . . getting to know each other. Finally there is a formal congregational vote to ratify the search committee's choice."

It's a bit more cumbersome than having a bishop make the appointment, but it is a process carefully calibrated to preserve two vital traditions: that of congregational polity and that of a learned clergy. David Pohl, who was with the Department of Ministry for twenty-two years, comments, "Training, credentialing, settlement, and support of our ministers—to me those are necessarily associational functions. No one congregation can provide for the support of our retired ministers and their survivors. No one congregation can train our ministers. And no one congregation can do anything about screening, psychological evaluations, about ethical professional standards, about gathering and disseminating the necessary information."

Pohl deserves much of the credit for professionalizing the process and establishing a core curriculum. Before the MFC, there were only regional committees, which did not always apply consistent standards, and the wooers and the wooed often met at General Assemblies, turning them into little better than meat markets. Pohl remembers that back when he was a candidate, careers were often jeopardized by breaches of confidentiality. Once, for instance, he was asked to meet a search committee in a hotel room and while they were still in session, there was a knock on the door and a second applicant, and then a third, showed up. In another instance, the chair of a search committee "was running around, asking people for their opinions of a confidential list of candidates he had received from the department."

Now the matchmaking system is orderly and discreet, but as in marriage there is no predicting the outcome. Sometimes the parties love each other and the relationship lasts for years, sometimes they do little better than get along, and sometimes they don't get along at all, in which case another search is in order and the process begins again.

A CHANGING MINISTERIAL PROFILE

Today, there are more than fifteen hundred ministers in UU fellowship, more than at any other time in our history. At the 2000 GA in Nashville, Tennessee, eighty more received preliminary fellowship while forty-eight received final fellowship. A breakdown of these numbers is instructive. Of these new ministers, ninety-nine want a career in the parish ministry—six as ministers of religious education—plus twenty-three in community ministry.

Community ministry, while carried on in affiliation with a UU parish, involves such "detached" undertakings as serving as chaplains in hospitals or hospices, as community organizers, campus ministers, or as heads of homeless shelters. Recently, there has been a proposal to do away with the three tracks of academic preparation (parish, religious education, and community) and instead give every candidate the same basic preliminary fellowship and then require postgraduate work in preparation for one of the three specialties—much as in medical training one obtains an MD degree and then, through residency, prepares for a specialty. No decision has yet been made regarding this proposal.

Another option is interim ministry. There are now eighty-five interim ministers, up from just forty-one less than ten years ago. These are people who have had previous permanent settlements and now serve congregations that have not completed the search process or need a healing transition after a long-term ministry or a traumatic parting of the ways. The term of service of interim ministers is clearly defined, and they agree not to apply for the permanent position.

More significant than numbers is the striking change in gender balance in the UU ministry. Two-thirds of those receiving fellowship in Nashville were women, and women now make up just about half of all active UU ministers, compared with virtually none in 1961 and a negligible two percent in the early 1970s. But we seem to have reached the peak of the wave. The presidents of both seminaries—William Murry of Meadville/Lombard and Rebecca Parker of Starr King—report that after a surge that for a while made female students the majority, the proportion of entering students has now leveled off at roughly half and half.

Another trend, but one that may also have peaked, is for most entering students to be second-career people, an unheard-of phenomenon before the 1960s, but almost universal in the following three decades. People switching from other pursuits are still preponderant among the applicants—an estimated 80 percent at Meadville/Lombard—but a few are once again showing up right out of college or graduate school.

Diane Miller, head of the Department of Ministry and a candidate for the UUA presidency in the 2001 election, has suggested that the timing of the entry of women into ministry is no accident. It happened during the Civil War, she says, when men were off fighting and dying, and again after the Vietnam War for the opposite reason. "During the war, theological schools were pumped up with many men seeking draft deferments," she observes, "but as soon as the draft went away they left the schools, leaving openings for women." Of course, the coming of the women's movement also played a role; indeed, Miller herself helped to form the Ministerial Sisterhood of Unitarian Universalists, and later served on the UUA's committee to promote affirmative action for women in ministry.

Have women made a difference? Miller thinks that the expectation that women are more nurturing, warmer, more caring, has been overblown. "There may be some truth to that," she comments, "but it's an odd stereotype," and she points to her own ministry, which has emphasized institutional strength and growth. "Other people have said that women are more oriented toward ritual, toward liturgy, toward community and less toward the pulpit. Personally, I don't get it."

Paul Johnson, on the other hand, from his perspective of twenty years in leadership, including the presidency, of the Unitarian Universalist Ministers Association, thinks that women have contributed at least in part to today's greater emphasis on spirituality, on "worship and ritual, on the inner life and right brain experience, though interest in the mind and rationality, and interest in social justice, remain very strong." But he doesn't believe the new concerns come only from the women; they also reflect a generational change. For instance, newcomers to our faith have lately not been primarily rebels against the dogmatism of a previous religious affiliation. Today they are often unchurched people who want "a sense of connection to the cosmos, an acknowledgement of mystery." He considers the trend positive "as long as we don't lose our bedrock commitment to the role of reason." This new emphasis is also reflected among ministers, both in response to their congregants' needs and because they, themselves, share their attitudes.

It is hard to say what is cause and what is effect—or if indeed there is a causal relationship—but coupled with these changes there is an apparent greater commitment to institutional loyalty and a lessening of divisiveness and personal self-indulgence. Johnson, for instance, has observed a fading of the anticlericalism that was a hallmark of many of the early fellowships: They either decided to call a minister or disappeared. What everyone hopes will also fade away is the issue of ministerial sexual misconduct that shook the denomination, especially during the years of the so-called sexual revolution. (David Pohl had to deal with eighteen such cases in his last five years as head of the Department of Ministry.)

Such renewed attention to institutionalism is also being observed at the schools for the ministry. The emphasis at Meadville/Lombard, President William Murry explains, is shifting from the academic more to the art and practice of ministry, reflecting, he says, the expectations of UU congregations. Most of them no longer want sermons that are highly philosophical or theological. "They want sermons that deal with personal fulfillment." As for Starr King, according to President Rebecca Parker, the school is doing a better job of preparing students for the parish ministry than it did ten years ago, accompanied by a modest trend to greater institutional commitment on the part of the students.

Meanwhile, both schools have successfully embraced human diversity in terms of sexual orientation, but racial diversity has

132 / PRESERVING THE FUTURE

not yet been achieved. There are now only some forty people of color in the UU ministry, and not all of them are active.

Among other recent trends, there are now more co-ministries: partners (sometimes married, sometimes not) sharing pulpits or splitting pastoral responsibilities in other ways. Second, there is a perception by some observers that there is a trend toward more denominational oversight (Pohl's intervention in the sexual misconduct fracas being one example), which at times creates a feeling that the UUA bureaucracy is intruding beyond its proper bounds. A more recent example is the suggestion floated by the Ministerial Fellowship Committee but not acted upon that only fellowshipped ministers be ordained by congregations, which would fly in the face of a basic denominational tradition. A more unifying observation, however, is that *theological* tensions have lessened.

BUDGETS IN BALANCE

Fortunately, so have some of the fiscal tensions.

The turning point came when Gordon McKeeman, while president of Starr King, realized that its budget had been balanced in large part by woefully underpaying the faculty. Apart from the question of fairness, he worried that once the then-current instructors retired, it would be just about impossible to replace them at those salary levels. Together with one of his board members, he met with David Osborne, the minister of the UU Congregation of Shelter Rock, and congregational leaders at their beautiful new location to make a plea for help in building an endowment fund. (Having outgrown its Plandome church and unable to expand because of building regulations, the congregation had bought an estate on nearby Shelter Rock Road and changed its name accordingly.)

After several more meetings and much internal discussion, the congregation in 1983 agreed to established a Trust for Theological Education with an endowment that eventually totaled $9 million. The UUA used the funds to provide support for both Starr King and Meadville/Lombard, with a lesser amount going to Harvard. Some of the money was initially used by the UUA for an independent study program it had set up to prepare candidates for ministry of religious education. When this program failed to get Massachusetts state approval for the granting of degrees, it was transferred to Meadville/Lombard in 1992, where it continues as its Modified Residency Program. The title "modified" refers to the fact that students are campus residents only during four January periods, while the rest of the year they engage in distance learning. Initially intended only for religious educators, the program now covers all three ministerial tracks, with half of the candidates currently enrolled preparing to work in RE, and one-fourth each preparing for either the parish or community ministries. Harvard, with lots of money of its own, has used its grants to set up a scholarship fund for UU ministerial students, matching the UUA contributions two-for-one. In addition, Veatch funds make possible a program of continuing education.

But while the schools may no longer face quite such acute money problems, that unfortunately is not true of many of the students. Scholarship help, though better than it was, is still inadequate, and some new ministers start their careers with debts ranging anywhere from $30,000 to an incredible $90,000. Repayment of such student loans is apt to drain twenty to twenty-five percent of their income—income that often isn't all that great to begin with. This also explains why such a high percentage go to non-denominational schools: Education is cheaper close to home.

Ralph Mero, a former parish minister who now heads the Office of Church Staff Finances, not only has responsibility for all UUA pension and group insurance plans, but works with district compensation consultants who, in turn, advise congregations about fair employment practices. Often, Mero points out, salaries and benefits are not at all appropriate. In fact, "we have lost ground over the last forty years in the relative compensation of ministers with their parishioners." One reason is, he says, that our growth has been "horizontal"—that we have many more smaller congregations. "In 1895 the average Unitarian congregation had 250 members. A hundred years later, the average UU congregation had 150 members," and such smaller societies usually have "an extremely difficult time paying a fair level of professional compensation." The rising tide of denominational fundraising, he concludes, "does not lift boats that have holes in the bottom—and many of our congregations still have holes in their financial bottoms."

In addition, while some congregations make generous contributions to pension plans, others do not, leaving some retired ministers trying to live on only about a $1,000 per month pension, plus their Social Security. It all comes back, he feels, to our reluctance to talk about money, especially to ask people to leave bequests to their church or the UUA in their wills. "The fundamental issue is that if you don't ask you don't receive," Mero concludes.

Perhaps, another forty years hence, we will be able to say that we not only have highly motivated, highly educated ministers, but that we show that we value their services by treating them more fairly. After all, despite our tradition of ministering to one another, it is primarily to our professional leaders that we look for help (in the words of McKeeman in his book of meditations) in "celebrating the triumphs of the human spirit, the miracles of birth and life, the wonders of devotion and sacrifice."

THE EDUCATORS' PERSPECTIVE

Numbers, procedures, and finances are all important, but ultimately what matters about ministers (and, indeed, about the laity) are the beliefs they bring to their calling.

After ten years as head of a UU seminary, Rebecca Parker observes that the hot topic of a decade ago—the tension between historic humanists and the "young Turks" who stressed spirituality—has been mostly resolved by an awareness that the core belief, the central tradition that makes us distinctive, is the humanist spirit. "That is the strength of Unitarian Universalism. The regard for human beings and the confidence and trust in our capacities as human beings gives us a sense of hope, and it is also where our concern about social justice comes from—this regard for the sacred worth of human beings, indeed of all life."

President William Murry of Meadville/Lombard agrees. The prevalent tension of some ten years ago between humanism and spirituality has ebbed, he says, estimating that today's students fall into three fairly equal groups: humanist, theist, and the ones he calls "universalist."

Parker goes on to point out that the UUA Principles and Purposes articulate a covenant that holds us all together. If there is tension now, she feels, it is between that sense of community and an "atomized" pluralism. "How do we allow the particularity, the personal freedom and diversity we value without [what we stand for] becoming flattened out?" she asks. The answers we develop are critical because "we are often just a little bit ahead of where the culture is, and in the American context we are also struggling with the breakdown of the old image of an America where people assimilate yet maintain a sense of community, that honors diversity yet is greater than the sum of its parts." Reflecting on these issues she concludes, "The reintroduction of language of the covenant is a theologically brilliant move.... It creates common ground by the things we shake hands on." It is a vision that a small group of dedicated Unitarian Universalist educators strive tirelessly to pass on to the next generation of religious leaders.

WELCOMING THE NEXT GENERATION

It is needful to transmit the passwords from generation to generation.

Antoine St. Exupery, no. 649

Just suppose: if over the past forty years, in addition to attracting new members—it is estimated that 85 to 90 percent of Unitarian Universalists today were not raised as such—we had been able to keep all our grown children as part of the UU family. We would be at least twice as numerous (and influential) as we are now. The fact that we do not retain the institutional loyalty of so large a proportion of our young people is particularly ironic in light of the fact that so many of our new members come to us specifically to find religious education programs for their children that reflect their own values.

The fault may lie with the ambivalence Unitarian Universalists so often feel not about their faith but about the structure that supports it. *Extension* is okay; *evangelism* is not. *Adequate funds for programs* are wonderful; *asking for them* is embarrassing. So it is with the way we raise our children. *Education* is good; *indoctrination* is bad. Unfortunately, in drawing the line between these extremes, we have all too often leaned over backwards not to impart to the next generation the need to undergird ideals with structure, with the result that our children may share our ideals in the abstract, but feel no loyalty to the institution that gives them viability.

Our confusion may well go back to William Ellery Channing's widely quoted affirmation that "The great end in religious instruction . . . is not to stamp our minds irresistibly upon the young but to stir up their own . . . not to give them a definite amount of knowledge but to inspire a fervent love of truth; not to form an outward regularity, but to touch inward springs." (Hence the name of *Inward Springs,* a periodical for liberal religious families, published under the auspices of the Unitarian Universalist Church of All Souls of New York City.) The problem is that if the young go through Sunday school without acquaintance with Unitarian Universalism, this is not a source to which their love of truth is likely to direct them.

The decision as to what to teach in Sunday school rests, of course, with the local congregations, but it is UUA curricula that provide them with their resources, and looking back at the learning modules of the 1950s and 1960s, it is striking how well they teach "the UU way of life," but how little they do to make explicit that this *is* the UU way. Tolerance, respect for other faiths, generosity, and sharing—these values come through clearly, but the benefit of celebrating and preserving them in community is left unsaid.

A NEW APPROACH IN RELIGIOUS EDUCATION

In recent years, there has been a conscious effort to bridge this gap, without for a moment weakening the emphasis on the teaching of values. Currently, the Department of Religious Education is developing a comprehensive lifespan curriculum series for children and youth (and also adults) that covers UU identity and history, Jewish and Christian heritage, other faiths, and social justice—the fundamental themes of UU religious education. There will be particular emphasis on providing age-appropriate help in answering that tongue-tying question, "What do you mean you're a Unitarian Universalist? Is that like the Moonies?" One new program for teenagers is quite specifically called "Articulating (Y)Our Faith."

Judith Frediani, director of curriculum development in the Department of Religious Education, has been involved in RE since 1973 and has worked for the UUA since 1985. Those years give her an unusual perspective on the changing emphases in what we teach our children. "The major themes of curricula say a lot about where the denomination is," she points out. In the 1960s and 1970s there was a secular, almost an anthropological approach. We taught children and youth about human beings as culture builders, as meaning makers, trying to nurture tolerance and appreciation of people all over the world. Because of a conscious decision to develop curricula that could be sold to public schools, they didn't even mention the UUA as publishers.

"Parents came back to us to say that their kids now knew more about Buddhism than about Unitarian Universalism," Frediani says. "In the 1980s, the Futures Committee wrote a report that said the clearest message they had received was that people wanted materials on UU identity. Then the new Principles and Purposes were adopted, and that fit in very nicely with the mission to focus on UU identity, UU history, and UU beliefs and values."

In the 1990s there was another shift, or rather two additional layers of concern: an attempt to answer questions about spiritual needs, and more emphasis on social justice and anti-racism. "People were asking, What makes us religious? So we developed curricula such as 'On the Path, Spirituality for Youth and Adults,' and we worked closely with the Faith in Action staff on issues of diversity and social action."

A comparison of the two courses on human sexuality—the first one published in 1971, the new one in 1999—shows how the denomination has moved from a primarily secular to a more religious emphasis. While both teach basic factual knowledge and acceptance of the varieties of sexual orientation, the earlier one tries hard not to be directive. The new curriculum, as the very name *Our Whole Lives* suggests, takes a more holistic view of sexuality in line with UU Principles, to teach not only facts about anatomy and human development, but to help clarify values, build interpersonal skills, and to create an understanding of the spiritual, emotional, and social aspects of sexuality. The four basic values it takes as its lodestones are self-worth, sexual health, responsibility, and justice, offering participants at each of five age-group levels information about sexual abuse, exploitation, and harassment, and showing parents how to participate constructively in the sexuality education of their children. By the end of 2000, more than three hundred congregations had already trained teachers to use the new curriculum.

This change in emphasis reflects the greater awareness of the spiritual dimensions of life that now characterizes the denomination. Now even most humanists acknowledge (and talk about) an interest in spirituality, and so do those who identify themselves as pagans, Buddhists, Goddess worshipers, Wiccans, etc. The Department of Religious Education has responded to this diversity by endeavoring to produce "mainstream" materials that are respectful of all beliefs without actively promoting any one of them. Of course that doesn't please everyone. "It's a balancing act," Frediani admits, noting that at various times such groups as UU Christians and lately some humanists have felt that their beliefs were insufficiently represented, but she adds, "We make every effort to acknowledge our diversity." And, of course, local congregations are always free to supplement the UUA curricula with their own materials, to substitute their own creations or those acquired from outside sources. But by and large, congregations seem happy with what they can obtain from "25."

Another fairly recent addition to the way the denomination is helping maintain high standards in religious education is the appointment of district RE consultants, who run training sessions for teachers, are available for consultation, and give courses on new curricula. They are paid partly by the districts and partly (through a Veatch grant) by the UUA. The Veatch program has also made money available for grants to congregations that make a commitment to raise salaries for their religious educators.

A NEW MINISTRY

No matter how good, however, no curriculum by itself is going to teach even a single child. Effectiveness in the classroom depends on teachers, and since teachers are almost universally volunteers, how good a job they do is in large measure dependent on the congregation's director (or minister) of religious education. And in those two parenthetical words there lies another story.

A book by Joan Goodwin aptly entitled *Giving Birth to Ourselves* tells that story in detail. Forty years ago, there was no such thing as a minister of religious education in our denomination. Although the Liberal Religious Educators Association (LREDA), founded in 1949, had established membership qualifications and codes of professional conduct, it wasn't until 1967 that the UUA began extending credentials to religious educators. This meant that even those RE directors who had academic training—and many were and still are locally recruited lay volunteers—felt they were second-class citizens compared with ordained ministers. The fact that almost all of them were women reinforced this perception on both sides.

The wall began to crumble in 1973 when the newly created Council on Ministerial Education included a LREDA representative. The notion of extending fellowship to religious educators began to be seriously discussed, and the 1979 General Assembly gave final approval (by a very slim margin) to a bylaws amendment providing that "fellowship may be for the purposes of parish ministry, the ministry of education or both, as determined by the action of the Ministerial Fellowship Committee." This was followed by the establishment of the UUA's independent study program for religious educators, but since it could not confer degrees, that still left one step before the hierarchical gap in professional leadership could be bridged, a step that was taken with the transfer of the program to Meadville/Lombard. As Goodwin reports, "Many dedicated full-time professionals seized the opportunity to move on to Ministry of Religious Education as soon as that option became available." Many smaller and midsize congregations, of course, still rely (and usually quite successfully) on part-time directors of religious education who may or may not have academic training.

YOUTH AND YOUNG ADULTS

The importance of keeping future generations connected with our movement doesn't end with Sunday school graduation. In fact, that's when the challenge really becomes acute: when parental influence fades and young people make independent decisions as to which church, if any, to attend. The UUA's resolve to help make it a smooth transition had its ups and downs, to say the least.

Beginning with Dana Greeley, an astonishingly high percentage of our leaders have formed their denominational ties as officers of youth organizations. And not only people in official positions, but many of our most distinguished ministers and lay leaders look back with fondness to their years as members of Liberal Religious Youth and its predecessor organizations. One of them is Wayne Arnason, co-minister at the West Shore UU Church in Cleveland, Ohio, UUA secretary, and trustee-at-large. Arnason has been active in many phases of denominational life over the years, and in telling the story of liberal religious youth organizations in a book he calls *Follow the Gleam,* he points out that such organizations have often created tensions within their denominations. When, for instance, three nineteenth-century Universalist ministers set about starting a national youth organization, they found that "discouragements of all sorts came upon us. . . . it was bringing in unorthodox methods and would teach young people cant and hypocrasy [sic]." That such attitudes would prevail even then is particularly striking because in those days "youth" generally meant under thirty-five, and youth leaders tended to be in their early thirties.

By the 1920s, the average age had dropped to the twenties, and when Liberal Religious Youth was formed through the precedent-setting merger of the Universalist Youth Fellowship and American Unitarian Youth in 1951, the accepted age range was fifteen to twenty-five, while the leadership clustered just north and south of twenty.

By this time, "youth autonomy" (perceived, ironically, by some later LRY leaders as adult abandonment) had become both a slogan and a goal, and LRY's executive director, Bill Gold, observed that many of the most devoted activists on the continental scene had never had the experience of belonging to a strong local group. "To them," he wrote, "[LRY] is a source of security in their eccentricity. This is a valuable contribution the group should make to youth who might otherwise be lonely in their individuality, but if it is the dominant force in the life of the group . . . it results in a distorted concept of LRY's program and purposes." These problems, according to Arnason, continued to exist in 1980 when he was consultant on youth programs for the UUA.

At the time of consolidation, the LRY executive director became part of the staff of the new UUA Division of Education, working with an advisory committee of adults. Soon, of course, the infamous 1960s arrived, and to the mix of eccentricities were added the combustible elements of drug and sexual experimentation. In addition, the political activism that swept through the younger generation became highly visible at the 1969 General Assembly when some thirty LRY delegates joined in voluble coalition with supporters of the Black Affairs Council. Shocked adult delegates went home to report that LRY "hippies" had seized the microphones and had camped out in the lobby of a downtown hotel. Even before the GA, an LRY president is quoted by Arnason as saying: "LRYers across the continent are uncomfortable with much that the denomination represents: its rationalism, its lack of symbolism, its [lack of] relevance to the lives of LRYers. By the mere fact of our dissatisfaction we have a role to play. The role of catalyst, agitator, and perhaps a vanguard."

The point about being a vanguard was prescient. Larry Ladd, who was LRY president in 1969 is now the UUA's financial advisor; Bill Sinkford, who held the presidency from 1965 to 1966, is a UUA department head and candidate for the presidency in the 2001 elections. Some LRY leaders, by the way, were not unmindful of the risks posed by the dubious reputation youth meetings and conferences were gaining. Ladd recalls the strong efforts the continental leadership was making to ban drugs at

LRY conferences, and Sinkford has been memorialized by what became known as the "Sinkford Sex Survey," a well-intentioned research project designed to give both local and continental leadership a sense of where members' values and sexual attitudes were moving.

But problems persisted. At the 1967 Continental Conference four delegates were caught smoking marijuana. It was the last night of the conference, so it was too late to toss them out. Says Arnason, "Finally it was decided to bring the matter up for the whole conference to talk about. . . . The air was full of stories of a wonderful renaissance happening among young people all over the country. How could a few LRYers possibly shatter that feeling by doing something they had been told would threaten the very existence of LRY as an organization?" The decision was to ask them to write letters to the LRY board reflecting on what they had done. Despite these efforts, the LRY's growing negative reputation did indeed threaten its survival. Parents began to pull their kids out of the organization; congregations disaffiliated their youth groups. When LRY's leaders, getting into the spirit of the times, drafted a Youth Agenda that demanded $100,000 from UUA for youth programs, "the reaction in the churches," in Arnason's words, "went all the way from disbelief and hostility through cautious support to boredom."

Perhaps it was boredom that drove the final nail. In any case, by the 1970s the organization was unraveling. Membership was in serious decline; there was no longer any staff support so that LRY events were completely youth run (and badly run, says Arnason); in any case, the "youth culture" had about run its course. In 1976, the UUA board established a special committee on youth programs to study LRY and make recommendations "as to the best ways for the UUA to develop, offer and support programs for youth generally of high school age." In 1979, in line with the committee's recommendations, a youth office was established and Arnason became the first full-time adult working on youth programming at UUA headquarters in ten years. It was time to turn over a new leaf.

THE NEW LEAF

In response to a joint recommendation from the administration and LRY, the UUA board voted to hold a Youth Assembly in 1981. Called "Common Ground," the assembly (as reported in a *Common Ground* publication) was attended by 179 youth and 65 adult delegates, plus 30 staff members. The districts having been asked to sponsor their own preparatory youth assemblies, twenty-three districts, plus five affiliated UU organizations, were represented. Clearly, this was a truly denomination-wide effort to think through how best to address such issues as (1) which age group a UU youth organization should serve, (2) its purposes and values, (3) its programs, (4) its name, (5) its funding, and (6) how it should relate to the UUA.

Key recommendations were to dissolve LRY and set up a new organization to serve youth from twelve to twenty-two years. Within this organization, there were to be separate programs for the junior high, high school, and post-high school years. Also, the group was to be clearly identified as a UU organization, served by both adult and youth staff, to be headquartered at 25 Beacon Street. A further recommendation for youth representation on the UUA board was turned down. The LRY board voted to dissolve, throwing its support to the new organization.

At a second youth assembly the following year there was a dedication service for "the new child in our midst" that pledged, "We welcome this child into the history of Unitarian Universalism and promise and engage that we will give her our guardian love and care." One bylaw provision was to define an adult "as someone over the age of twenty-two." A more instrumental vote was to adopt the name Young Religious Unitarian Universalists, known by its acronym of YRUU, pronounced "Why are UU." As Wayne Arnason points out, this double meaning was intentional. "Why are you *you*? This is *the* question that young people ask themselves as they enter that period of their lives most involved with seeking a personal identity." And of course: "Why are you Unitarian Universalist?" The need to make their UU identity explicit was a continuous and universally agreed-on theme in all four days of the conference.

Also significant was the decision that the governing council should have twenty-six youth members (twenty-three representing the districts, plus three at large), as well as eight adults, including a UUA board representative. "Youth autonomy" was no longer a pressing issue, at least with those attending the conferences. Those who participated in the process saw it as a passing of the torch, while at least some of those who only found out about it later felt that the torch had been ripped from their hands. Very likely this difference in perception is another symptom of the disconnectedness between LRY continental leadership and local groups that had occurred in the 1970s and that had so much to do with the organization's troubles and demise.

The unfortunate result, as Jennifer Harrison, then an LRYer and now UUA's youth program director, points out is that between 1973 and 1978 we lost much of our youth leadership. The easy transition from youth to denominational involvement was severed and had to be patiently rebuilt.

YRUU TODAY

Twenty years later it is clear that the founders of YRUU did their job well. The name, the structure, the policies have all endured, and the growing number and enthusiasm of youth delegates at General Assemblies provide testimony to the organization's success. There are now some fifteen thousand names on the mailing list of *Synapse*, YRUU's twice-yearly publication, and reports reaching the UUA Youth Office indicate that congregational youth programs are growing at a rapid pace.

The main emphasis of the youth office is on programs that train both youth leaders and youth group advisors: leadership development conferences, spirituality development conferences, and advisor training programs. The headquarters staff invites teams of trainers—made up of both youth and adults, often ministers—and they in turn organize conferences in their districts. They also work closely with district youth advisory committees. Jennifer Harrison considers the spirituality workshops particularly significant because of the difference between youth and adult worship. "Corporate worship in the congregational setting is very much a matter of people sitting facing forward to listen to a speaker. But in youth worship, everyone participates . . . sitting in a circle, and spontaneity is an important element. The whole idea of the spirituality development conferences is to try to break down some of the barriers between adult- and youth-style worship—for the adults to see the validity and depth of the spiritual exploration of our youth."

The YRUU Steering Committee annually selects two program specialists to work at the Youth Office for one year. Nathan Staples, one of the recent specialists, offers the additional observation that youth worship services are usually held at night, and that the dark is important to the sense of community that these services engender. Addressing the issue of the age span in YRUU—fourteen to twenty in some districts, fourteen or even twelve to twenty-two in others—Staples says, "I couldn't say exactly why it works, but it does. The older kids are kept in check by the younger ones, and the younger ones emulate the older ones. It's kind of a mentoring relationship, and it's just an amazing experience." Some districts have conferences for the entire age range where the older youths act in leadership positions and as role models; others prefer separate meetings for junior high, high school, and post-high school members; still others have both. The joint meetings work, Harrison explains, because there are very clear and strictly enforced behavior standards.

Staples, at twenty-two, again speaking from recent personal experience, explains, "Junior high is an especially hard time for Unitarian Universalists. There's a lot of peer pressure that doesn't match our standards. It was very important for me to see people in high school and college or even getting started on their careers who had made it."

The Internet has had a highly positive impact on youth involvement in the denomination, making it possible for the Youth Office to communicate with people all across the continent quickly and easily. (The director gets an average of seventy e-mails a day.) There is a YRUU website, a chat room, the youth council holds meetings in cyberspace, and anyone can download the program resources from a home computer.

The Youth Office also organizes a yearly social justice conference in Washington, DC, where YRUU delegates learn how to organize grassroots political campaigns and how to lobby their elected representatives. After a lull in the 1980s and early 1990s, there is once again a lively interest on the part of UU youth in social justice issues, and YRUU has pledged to become an antiracist organization, hoping that as a by-product it may also become more multicultural. In fact, because of inter-racial marriages and adoptions, and because members are more likely to invite their friends than grownups do, YRUU is already more multicultural than our adult denomination. Furthermore, Harrison describes YRUU as a "safe place" for gay, lesbian, and transgender youth in the difficult years of early or mid-adolescence.

The phrases that jump out at you in the responses to a questionnaire as to how YRUU has affected members' lives are: *amazing friends, incredible friends, spiritual realization, UU guidelines changed my way of thinking, helped me express my individuality, gave me a more positive outlook, gave me focus and responsibility, made my life really complete.* That beats any number of committee reports.

BEYOND HIGH SCHOOL

Hard figures are hard to come by, but we are still losing an estimated two-thirds of our young people once they reach college age. At least it's no longer for lack of trying. For one thing, many congregations conduct bridging ceremonies to mark the transition to young adulthood. Others are trying out evening services; a few are running coffee houses. And to encourage and support this revived interest, there is once again an active UUA young adult program.

At consolidation, the newly hatched UUA had a College Centers Office that was charged with supporting the work of the previously merged Channing-Murray Foundation, later renamed

Student Religious Liberals. By 1963, when Orloff Miller, a UU minister now retired, headed the office, there were one hundred campus groups. (Incidentally, Miller, who was one of James Reeb's companions when Reeb was killed in Alabama, recalls that the reason he, Reeb, and Clark Olsen were having that fateful dinner together was their common interest in campus ministry.) Five years later, however, the position was terminated, and for the next eighteen years, there was no UUA staff person assigned exclusively to programs for young adults.

The consequences were swift and painful. While in 1966 roughly one-fifth of the members of UU congregations were young adults, by 1983 the percentage had shrunk to only one out of ten—this at a time when persons between eighteen and thirty made up more than 20 percent of the population of the United States and Canada. With YRUU concentrating on a younger age group, President Eugene Pickett in 1985 recommended to the board the establishment of a Young Adult Ministries Task Force. The task force recommendations two years later started with an intriguing historical observation. When King John Sigismund of Transylvania issued his Act of Toleration he was twenty-eight. When James Freeman led his King's Chapel parishioners in rejecting the Trinity he was twenty-six. And when Ezra Gannett helped to found the American Unitarian Association and was elected its secretary he was twenty-four. They might have added that when Dana Greeley became minister of the then staid and conservative Arlington Street Church he was an astonishing twenty-six.

After casting an envious glance at what other denominations were doing, the task force recommended UUA support for the Continental UU Young Adults Network (C*UUYAN), which was just in the process of formation as the result of a young adult continental conference in 1986. The conference was also the occasion for the first Opus, the annual continental spiritual retreat for young adults. To secure funding, the task force submitted a grant proposal to—where else!—the Veatch program.

To provide staff support, the task force suggested the appointment of a young adult project coordinator in the

Department of Extension. The age group to be served was to be eighteen to thirty (since raised to thirty-five), intentionally providing a four-year overlap with YRUU. There followed many specific recommendations to provide resource materials, leadership training, and conferences to support this work.

The UUA Board's response reflected good intentions but sparse resources: in 1987 a quarter-time staff person was hired to administer grants to young adult and campus ministry groups. It took until 1994 before there was once again a full-time young adult/campus ministry director. Located in Princeton, New Jersey, as part of the UUA's current effort at staff decentralization, the Office of Young Adult/Campus Ministry oversees 125 campus programs and gives staff support to C*UUYAN, the General Assembly Young Adult Caucus, and the annual leadership and networking conferences. According to Donna DiSciullo, who heads the office, the campus groups are made up of about half "birthright" Unitarian Universalists and half of other students who are attracted to UU programs and beliefs. Most groups are solely student led—that is, there is no minister to support them. Recruiting more campus ministers is one of DiSciullo's prime objectives since without them the rapid turnover in student population makes the long-term survival of these groups highly problematical.

There is also a spiritual reason why a ministerial presence is important. It is DiSciullo's belief that campus ministry and young adult ministry should be worship centered, thus "creating a space where young adults can get in touch with their souls. From there flows the work of social justice, service, and inspiration." Lay-led worship services do not always succeed in meeting this need. On the other hand, when young adults attend congregational services they often miss the intimacy and power of the youth services they had experienced; also, they may see no one else their age.

The titles of a few of the resources available from the young adult/campus ministry office give a good indication of its range of activities. There is a monograph on "How to Start a Young Adult Group"; another on "Weaving Worship to Welcome Young Adults" into the life of a congregation. There is a "Youth and Young Adult Leadership School Handbook," as well as a campus ministry "Instant Start-up Kit" that includes suggested mission statements, newspaper ads, and program ideas. Its three-times-a-year newsletter called *Ferment*, together with its website, help to weave the young adult network together.

We no longer totally neglect our young adults but we are still a long way from doing all we can to let them know that they are welcome members of the UU family. While some churches in campus communities do their best to provide ministerial support, not all do, and few ministers can take the time from their parish obligations to do the job justice. "It's very hard to get congregations to think beyond the church walls," DiSciullo says. While money may not be the answer to all problems, it sure would help with this one.

Our Wider Horizons

THE EQUALITY CHALLENGE REVISITED

Love and truth shall meet; justice and peace shall embrace.

Chaim Stern, no. 633

In the words of Sophia Fahs, "Some beliefs are like walled gardens. They encourage exclusiveness, and the feeling of being especially privileged. Other beliefs are expansive and lead the way into wider and deeper sympathies."

Fahs, a renowned religious educator, pioneered the Beacon curriculum that introduced the principles of progressive education into Unitarian Sunday schools in mid-twentieth century. She was contrasting the openness of liberal religion with the rigidities of more orthodox faiths, and in terms of that comparison she was undoubtedly correct. Looking back, however, it is ironic to what an extent the Unitarianism (and to a lesser extent Universalism) of the time was also a "walled garden" whose adherents—predominantly white, well off, well educated—also felt "especially privileged," accepting, probably unconsciously, the biases of the larger culture.

WOMEN BREAK THE BARRIER

At the time of consolidation, it was simply taken for granted that men should be in charge. The original UUA bylaws consistently referred to all officers as "he." In 1967, a survey by the UU Committee on Goals found that 47 percent of Unitarian Universalists polled said that gender might hamper the effectiveness of a woman in the ministry (compared, intriguingly, with 27 percent who said so about blacks). That despite the boast that when Olympia Brown was ordained by the Universalists in 1863 she was the first woman to be so recognized by a North American ecclesiastical body.

The black empowerment movement of the 1960s did much to shake UU self-satisfaction, but it wasn't focused so much on creating greater diversity within the denomination as on aligning the UUA with outside social forces aimed at overcoming racial oppression. The first serious challenge to the barriers to full participation *within* our movement came later—from women. It was at their initiative, as part of the burgeoning women's movement in society at large, that beginning in the early 1970s the UUA board began to "desex" the bylaws, changing every "he" to "he or she."

Still it took until 1984 for the Principles and Purposes of the association to be made truly inclusive, and Diane Miller mentions that when she was ordained in the early 1970s, women made up only 2 percent of the UU clergy. (Today, women make up roughly half of active UU ministers and still represent two-thirds of the students in our theological schools, though their percentage of entering students has leveled off.) The same kind of imbalance prevailed among the professional staff at UUA headquarters, but that symptom of sexism, too, was successfully addressed, and Miller herself is now one of about a dozen senior staff members at 25 Beacon Street.

Not that there weren't some bumps along the way. Natalie Gulbrandsen recalls how annoyed many women were when President Paul Carnes named a Women in Religion Committee without bothering to consult the Women's Federation. And as Miller points out, while "we didn't have the barriers other denominations did, so we didn't have as many hurdles to break down, the biggest issue wasn't our female gender but our feminist approach to challenging institutions. Where in the past an exceptional woman might have slipped through the cracks, we were saying that the system had to change. We did not want to be put in gender-defined types of ministry; we wanted to have all types of ministry and to be leaders in our own right."

As part of this determination to change the system, these clerical pioneers formed MSUU (Ministerial Sisterhood Unitarian Universalists), which joined in a powerful coalition with the Women's Federation to dismantle the remaining barriers to full participation. One further indication of their success and of changing attitudes among men as well as women: our last three moderators—Sandra Caron, Natalie Gulbrandsen, and Denise Davidoff—have all been women. In 1985, Caron ran—though unsuccessfully—for the presidency, to be followed by two other women candidates: Carolyn S. Owen-Towle in 1993 and Diane Miller as this book goes to press. Both 2001 candidates for moderator are women, and women occupy some of our most prestigious pulpits. If we are still, more than we probably wish, privileged to be in a lovely garden, at least the gender balance inside the garden is now reflective of the face of humanity.

EQUAL RIGHTS FOR GAY, LESBIAN, AND TRANSGENDER PEOPLE

The next group to come knocking on our doors were gay men and lesbians.

During Robert West's tenure, UUA staff and programs—particularly those concerned with social responsibility and religious education—began to address gay and lesbian concerns. Then, in 1973, the General Assembly called for a separate headquarters Office of Gay Affairs (which has evolved into today's Office of Bisexual, Gay, Lesbian, and Transgender Concerns), and in 1975 West appointed Arlie Scott as its first director.

The office's change of name reflects a growing concern for the rights of people with minority sexual orientations, a concern that has often placed the UUA at the leading edge of social change. Barbara Pescan in her UUA pamphlet on this subject traces this expanding awareness through eleven resolutions adopted by General Assemblies over the years. As early as 1984, the UUA made history by voting to support ministers who were performing same-sex unions; in 1996 our commitment culminated in a General Assembly vote to support "legal recognition for marriage between members of the same sex." That same year, the UUA also recognized the need to attend to the concerns of transgender people. More significant than even the institutional response is the remarkably swift change in attitudes toward sexual orientation that—once again reflecting society, but as usual setting the pace—our denomination has undergone. One indication is the treatment of transgender issues in *Our Whole Lives*, our most recent sexuality curriculum. But probably the most radical impact has been on the nature of our ministry.

David Pohl, who spent twenty-two years with the Department of Ministry, serving first as settlement director then as its head, recalls helping to place the first two openly gay ministers in UU pulpits in 1980, when Douglas Morgan Strong went to Augusta, Maine, and Mark Belletini went to Hayward, California. "I was kind of proud of that," Pohl says, "proud of working with the churches and search committees that had the courage to make those decisions early on. However, it took us a bit longer—about four years—to place our first lesbian woman."

Strong's own recollection of this breakthrough reflects some of the personal anguish that was involved. "When I went before the MFC [Ministerial Fellowship Committee], I was petrified," he wrote in *First Days Record*. "Back then [in 1979], the number of out gay ministers successfully serving congregations was easy to count. There were none." He also points out that the GA vote in favor of the Office of Gay Affairs was by no means unanimous and that many voiced strong objection. "I recall one colleague asking the assembly if the next step would be an Office of Bestiality." Even after gaining his pulpit, it took Strong almost eighteen months to convince the editors of the *UU World* that AIDS was a topic worth covering. "There was a collective feeling," he claims, "that AIDS was not an appropriate topic for Unitarian Universalists to ponder."

Another personal story is that of Eugene Navias who wrote in the *UU World*, "When I applied for the job of director of the Religious Education Department, more than ten years had gone by since the first GA resolutions, and still I worried that the UUA would not appoint an openly gay man to a sensitive post involving the religious education of children and youth. So I went to Gene Pickett, the UUA president, to face the question before the day of my interview."

Pickett asked him what reactions he had had from people in the denomination. When Navias reported that the responses had all been positive, Pickett assured him that that was the way he felt, too.

"I was so choked up, grateful, relieved that I just mumbled some incoherent thanks and left," Navias concludes. "Bless Gene Pickett. I know of no other religious denomination in this society where that could have happened in 1982."

And Kim Crawford Harvie, senior minister of Boston's Arlington Street Church, has written, "I have been extraordinarily lucky. In living my life as an openly lesbian woman, I have gained far more—infinitely more—than I have lost. One factor tips the balance: I was raised as a Unitarian Universalist. I was raised with Sunday school lessons that taught the beauty of difference, in a faith which nurtures self-respect, dignity, and courage. . . . I know I am loved not in spite of who or what I am, but because of who and what I am. And that has made all the difference."

Strong, together with Carolyn McDade, went on to co-chair the Unitarian Universalists for Lesbian and Gay Concerns (now named Interweave), which in the early 1980s successfully applied for a Veatch grant for the first of the Lesbian and Gay Convocations that have met annually ever since. He also served on Common Vision, a UUA committee that developed the Welcoming Congregations Program which has sought to overcome the lingering resistance to the presence of gay men and lesbians not only in the pulpit but also in the pews. By the end of 1999, close to two hundred congregations had completed this program—roughly one out of five.

Another attempt to erase barriers of prejudice in our denomination has been the UUA's *Beyond Categorical Thinking* program. Triggered by incidents when gay or lesbian ministers were denied appointments once their sexual orientation became known, the program conducts workshops for search committees that address the entire range of discrimination, including not only bias based on sexual orientation but also on race, as well as the "stained glass ceiling" that has at times kept women from attaining the more prestigious pulpits. UU ministers have also been in the forefront of conducting same-gender services of commitment and union. At a time when some mainstream Protestant denominations are still agonizing about gender orientation issues, we can, in Strong's words, "stand proud and take a bow for the work we do."

The full significance of these changes is that they have been important not only to those who might previously have felt unwelcome or of lesser rank, but for the impact it has had on the denomination as a whole. After almost twenty years on headquarters staff, UUA executive vice president Kay Montgomery is in a good position to assess these changes, and she believes that they have made a huge difference in broadening our horizons. Referring to the entry of so many women into our ministry, she says: "People used to talk about 'the feminization of the ministry' as an expression of disapproval or anxiety. Now that phrase is used, if at all, only as a compliment. Another huge change has been the acceptance of open gays and lesbians into significant pulpits. Together these have been sea changes in terms of who we are." And Robert Senghas, from his perspective as executive vice president in the 1970s and currently a member of the board, observes as one symptom of the change that there is less tension between headquarters and parish ministers. That is due at least in part, he believes, to the fact that women have less of what he calls "an authority problem"—some men's tendency to chafe against perceived dominance—and are therefore less inclined to be suspicious of administration initiatives.

OPENING THE DOOR

We have less reason, however, to feel gratified about our success in fighting the racism of our culture or in attracting people of color to our congregations. One reason, probably, is that the pain of the BAC/BAWA controversy of the 1960s was slow to heal. In the words of Melvin Hoover, the African American minister who heads Faith in Action, the UUA Department for Diversity and Justice, "It took us nearly a decade to heal our wounds . . . to acknowledge our mistakes, renew our commitment, and sharpen our understanding about the 'new racism' of the 1980s."

So it was not until 1981 that the UUA Board adopted a resolution committing the association to seek to become "a racially equitable institution and . . . make an effective contribution toward achieving a similarly equitable society." Implementation began when the trustees contracted with Community Change, Inc., to conduct a racism audit of UUA headquarters. As described by Hoover in his chapter of the 1993 *Unitarian Universalist Pocket Guide*, this was followed by the formation of a series of task forces for monitoring institutional racism, and of a Black Concerns Working Group charged with cooperating with congregations and UU organizations in counteracting racism.

There was much to be done. With only a bare handful of ministers of color at the time of consolidation, the number in 1987 was still a meager fifteen. A 1988 audit revealed a similar lack of representation in the makeup of our congregations, and in response, the next year, the UUA published a curriculum by Mark Morrison-Reed, now co-minister in Toronto, on "How to Open the Door."

In 1992, President William Schulz called again for the denomination to increase its racial and cultural diversity, and the board set up a diversity task force. Executive vice president Kay Montgomery, having served under three presidents, sees the Schulz initiative as a reflection of his deepest personal commitments. "Most people experienced him as a very good public figure and spokesperson," she says, "but in his heart he is an activist." Having joined the UUA staff as Eugene Pickett's director of social concerns, Schulz followed Pickett as president, and when his two terms ended went on to become the head of Amnesty International USA. "His greatest strength as president," Montgomery believes, "is that he was pretty fearless in terms of issues of justice, even willing to lose big donors if that's what happened." However, Montgomery adds, initiatives that are perceived by congregations as "top-down" have a way of not going very far. "Change in our denomination almost always starts with some marginalized people creating enough discomfort so that they finally get the attention of people of influence. Then the board and the staff work out an initiative and become believers." That's what she believes took place when the 1992 Calgary General Assembly adopted a resolution that called on Unitarian Universalists to "support a vision of a Unitarian Universalist faith which reflects the reality of a racially diverse and multicultural global village," and charged the board of trustees with taking immediate steps to achieve these goals. The broad coalition that supported the resolution included, among others, the Coalition of African American UU Organizations, the Network of Black Unitarian Universalists, the Urban Church Coalition, as well as the ministers', women's, and youth organizations.

In response, the Association hired an interfaith consulting group, Crossroad Ministries, to help it develop a program of anti-racism training. The following year more than fifty UU leaders met in St. Louis and agreed that since integration and diversification efforts had not succeeded in ending racism, the denomination should focus on pursuing a program of active *anti*-racism. By 1996 these initiatives culminated in a report to the General Assembly entitled *Journey Toward Wholeness,* and in 1997 a new chapter in the UUA's struggle with racial issues was launched when the General Assembly resolved to commit itself to an "Anti-Racist Unitarian Universalist Association." The resolution urged all congregations and UU organizations to "develop an ongoing process for the comprehensive institutionalization of antiracism and multiculturalism, *understanding that whether or not a group becomes multiracial, there is always the opportunity to become antiracist"* (emphasis added).

In 1999, the Association stopped relying on Crossroads Ministries, adapting its training model so as to be more reflective of UU theology and led by UU trainers. But the purpose remained the same: to help UU congregations and organizations to become more inclusive, develop new relationships in our communities, and help both UU institutions and individuals to be more effective, authentic, and accountable to those who are oppressed. The opportunity to dismantle racism and oppression, as the Journey Toward Wholeness information packet puts it, would "help to move all of us closer to the wholeness we yearn for."

THE JOURNEY BEGINS

The Journey Toward Wholeness Transformation Committee's primary mechanism for achieving its goals is to conduct weekend workshops for denominational leaders that are geared to achieving the transformation of the participants . . . enabling them, in turn, to encourage comparable transformations in their home congregations.

The term *anti-racism* often causes some confusion among those invited to participate. "But I am not a racist," is a typical initial reaction, as people feel not only that they don't need such training but that the suggestion that they do is tantamount to an insult. In today's parlance, however, anti-racism signifies a commitment to dismantling the status quo that builds racism into our culture. It goes beyond tolerance to active efforts to reshape the structures of our society, finally replacing the racial oppression that has been endemic ever since Europeans began colonizing North America five centuries ago with an equally pervasive commitment to justice.

Overt examples of racial injustice—discrimination in housing, employment, and educational opportunities—are all widely recognized, but whites are often unaware of the more subtle humiliations. A single example may illustrate the point: a white customer can walk into a department store without giving a thought to being taken for a shoplifter; a person of color will feel—rightly or wrongly, but too often rightly—immediate apprehension that she/he is being watched or even followed by store security personnel. A more vicious example: racial profiling on the nation's highways, harassing people of color for "driving while black."

In an effort to create awareness of just how deeply racism is built into our social structure, the typical three-day workshop begins fairly dispassionately with a standard "big-sheets-on-the-wall" exercise. The sheets have four sections representing four periods in our history, starting in 1492 and ending with the present. In each time slot, participants are asked to write events that shaped our racist institutions on the top (from the Constitutional acceptance of slavery to the assault on affirmative action), and examples of resistance to racism (the march on Selma; hate crime legislation) on the bottom. The point is that it is difficult to comprehend the role of racism in our culture without an understanding of the conscious, intentional decisions that shaped and keep shaping it, or of the courageous, ongoing, often bitter struggle to resist it.

Subsequent exercises are designed to create an awareness of the ways in which the institutions and culture of our society provide power and privilege for white people—even those who think they harbor no prejudice. For instance, white participants are asked to list the ways in which the color of their skin has provided them, probably without their thinking about it, with advantages on a daily basis: living in whatever part of town they can afford, not having to wonder whether getting hired was a sign of tokenism, not having to explain to their children why some people call them names.

As the lessons sink in, participants begin to understand how systemic power turns latent attitudes into racism. They also develop an awareness that despite all their goodwill and good intentions, they have probably been part of the support system that has entrenched racism in our society, and they gain new insight into the relationship between racism and privilege.

Leon Spencer is one of the trainers for many of the workshops. A former member of the UUA Board of Trustees and professor at Georgia Southern University, he has honed his understanding of racism as both a scholar and an African American. He demonstrates that what makes racism so intractable is the white, middle-class fear that by coming to grips with it they might lose their identity and the privileges the culture has granted them. White people in the USA, he says, "don't want to think about racial issues, talk about them, or feel them. They fear that they might have to give something up."

That is why the workshops go on to a discussion of techniques for dismantling racism and what is involved in transforming the UUA into an anti-racist, multicultural institution. It is a transformation that progresses from symbolic change (adopting resolutions), to identity change (growing awareness), to structural change (audits and restructuring), culminating in becoming fully inclusive, characterized by a sense of restored community and mutual caring. Hence the name, "Journey Toward Wholeness."

HOW FAR HAVE WE COME?

The need for the program is well illustrated by an incident at the General Assembly of 1993, in Charlotte, North Carolina. The organizers thought it might be a clever idea to hold a Thomas Jefferson Ball to which delegates would come in colonial costume. They were greatly embarrassed, even stunned, when black Unitarian Universalists asked, "Should we come in chains?" It is this kind of "not thinking" about our culturally pervasive racism that the program is designed to overcome.

Is it working? So far not many congregations have experienced the two-and-a-half-day "Creating a Jubilee World" workshops. Melvin Hoover points out that the UUA's effort is so difficult because it is a first among all denominations. On the other hand, much energy has gone into transforming the UUA's institutional core and into refining the training of UU leaders, leading Moderator Davidoff to observe that it is extraordinary how much the training that the Board of Trustees underwent has become part of its culture.

Public recognition for the program came when former president Bill Clinton included four Unitarian Universalists among the 150 religious leaders invited to the White House to discuss his "One America" initiative. Eunice Benton, Mid-South District executive, was quoted in *Faith in Action*, the department's newsletter, as saying, "Of all the images of that day, none is more memorable for me than the marvelous spectrum of raiment and faces gathered in the East Room. . . . This was not a collection of white folks in white collars!" Significantly, "President Clinton suggested that training, not just good intentions, will be necessary if racism is to be overcome. He observed that while many people of good intent desire to make things better, doing the work of defeating racism will require that people train themselves. . . . I was proud to know that there were four of us Unitarian Universalists included in this gathering." Another of the four, Robette Dias, one of only two Native Americans present at the meeting and a program associate for the Department of Faith in Action, was impressed by Clinton's acknowledgment that he had at first been "tone deaf" to the concerns of Native Americans but had learned a great deal since then. Indeed, "tone deaf" seems like a great phrase to describe our society's (and more than we care to admit our denomination's) response to racism, for how can you tackle a problem whose existence you don't acknowledge, only partly understand, or possibly are even unaware of?

Meanwhile, the UUA has also published a curriculum on *Weaving the Fabric of Diversity* and another on *The Welcoming Congregation*. Institutional measures now include, by way of example, a line for comments about each employee's anti-racism efforts in the annual performance evaluation form.

Not that there aren't also skeptics.

Thandeka, a distinguished UU theologian of color, conducted a workshop at the 1999 GA provocatively entitled "Why Anti-racism Will Fail." Her main point is that it is class and not race bias that makes the problem so intractable. Another critique was published by Tom Schade, associate minister at the First Unitarian Church of Worcester, Massachusetts, in the Summer 2000 issue of *UU Voice*. "In a religious body that will not insist on a single definition of the holy, or of worship, or of God," he writes, "we insist on a single definition of the most complex aspect of our social system," which leads him to conclude that the program is guilty of "coercive organizing."

One point that probably no one would question is that racism is indeed, as Schade says, the most complex—and likely the most poisonous—aspect of our social system. And while we may disagree about methodology, we can all be responsive to Emerson's caution that "what you are . . . thunders so that I cannot hear what you say."

We have, indeed, been saying the right things for many decades, yet what we are is still a far from multicultural denomination, and one whose effectiveness in fighting racism is at best sporadic. Emerson's challenge would therefore seem due for some attention. *Journey Toward Wholeness* is a bold attempt to change what we *are*.

Summing up what we have achieved and what still needs to be done, President John Buehrens says, "We have a common commitment to anti-racism at the level of the Association's leadership, which has encouraged more people of color to give us a try again. The real work, however, will take place at the level of congregational and individual consciousness, and that part of the road will be long, bumpy—and yet an exciting spiritual journey."

LIVING UP TO A PROUD TRADITION

The struggle to end racial injustice is by no means the UUA's only effort to shape a society more reflective of our ideals and aspirations. That commitment, a central part of our historic heritage, was woven into the new denomination's fabric right from the time of its founding, when the resolutions adopted at the founding General Assembly included concern about capital punishment, racial discrimination, nuclear disarmament, mental health, and migratory workers. No wonder GA delegates ever since have had a sense of déjà vu.

Also, since the decision to preserve the autonomy of the Service Committee left the UUA without direct involvement in social action, President Greeley quickly established a headquarters Department of Social Responsibility. That parallel pattern has been preserved to the present, and while the proud story of the Service Committee represents a major element of the denomination's social witness, it is not part of the organizational history of the UUA, hence of this book. It probably deserves a volume unto itself.

As the first director of social responsibility, Homer Jack devoted considerable effort to the civil rights struggle in the South and to promoting nuclear disarmament and world peace. Toward the end of his tenure he, like the whole denomination, was swept up by the black empowerment controversy.

Soon thereafter, the need to whip the budget into balance required that the department be consolidated with others, but that did not end such social action and political policy activities as the Social Action Clearing House, the Social Responsibility Office in Washington, the Office on Aging, or the publication of the Pentagon Papers, which represented an all-time landmark in the defense of freedom from government repression.

When the financial crunch eased, Paul Carnes was able to reestablish an independent Office of Social Responsibility and recruited William Schulz to head it. When Eugene Pickett, upon Carne's death, succeeded him as president, he named Schulz as his executive vice president. Pickett's biographer, Tom Owen-Towle, quotes Pickett as saying in 1980 that the need was both to create a world without war, and to rebuff "the emergent new right in its vengeful desire to smother the rights of women, gay people, minorities, and others who struggle for justice." He, in effect, set the agenda for the denomination as he called on it to support "Black rights, Chicano rights, and Indian rights; women's rights and gay rights; workers' rights and veterans' rights; children's rights and students' rights; welfare rights and tenants' rights; the rights of the elderly and the rights of the handicapped."

Reflecting our commitment to the inherent worth and dignity of every person, it is an agenda that serves as well today as it did then, and unless the metaphorical millennium follows the real one, will presumably continue to serve for some generations to come. It is an agenda that, over the years, has led to the creation at various times of a variety of departments and offices, including the Department for Social Justice, the Office for Racial and Cultural Diversity, the Office for Bisexual, Gay, Lesbian and Transgender Concerns, as well as the Washington, DC, office. Under President John Buehrens all these agencies were consolidated under a single umbrella—Faith in Action: A UUA Department for Diversity and Justice.

At UUA headquarters, the Faith in Action staff is primarily engaged in helping UU congregations implement the social witness positions adopted at General Assemblies and conducting periodic advocacy and training conferences. Meanwhile the location of the Washington office positions it to respond to legislative and public policy issues that reflect our justice agenda, relying heavily on coalition building. In pursuit of an overall, long-term strategy designed to dismantle systemic oppression, the two offices between them:

- Provide staff support for the Association's anti-racism programs, including Journey Toward Wholeness.
- Implement the Welcoming Congregation Program by, for instance, publishing the *Welcoming Congregation Handbook,* which suggests ways in which congregations can tackle bisexual, gay, lesbian, and transgender issues.
- Support legislation in favor of campaign finance reform, church-state separation, reproductive freedom, and economic, racial, and gender identity justice.

Because staff limitations require careful setting of priorities, the DC office has to be content with signing on to coalitions or submitting advocacy letters on other issues that are of just as much concern, such as peace and disarmament, gun violence, and the environment. However, it also stands ready to speak out when critical issues suddenly hit the headlines, such as hate crimes and freedom-threatening far right legislation.

Social justice is also a major concern of YRUU and of the campus and young adult groups. A good way to find out more about their programs is to access their websites, as is also true of the Washington office and of the UUA's Social Witness Commission. The bulk of the denomination's social action work is carried out at the local level by congregations and districts; in addition, consideration time at each General Assembly is taken up by consideration of statements of conscience—resolutions dealing with social concerns.

These yearly GA resolutions reconfirm our historic commitment to peace and justice. Unitarian Universalists are justifiably proud of the reforms which were spearheaded by people of our faith, and the implied promise we make when we claim this tradition is that we will try to live up to it. Having just survived what may justly be called the Century of the Concentration Camp, observing a world beset by brutality, civil wars, and the needless suffering caused by runaway greed, we are painfully aware that it is not an easy challenge, but equally aware that the need to do so is more essential than ever.

Our efforts are no longer based on the easy assumption that the underlying impetus of human history is "onward and upward forever." Still, some undying hope keeps us from giving up. Perhaps the words of Charles Darwin—not so incidentally himself a Unitarian—are more in line with what is now the basis of our conviction that social witness matters. According to Darwin, the world is "in its own way, contingently hospitable." The challenge is to make it more so, for as many people and other living things as possible. Which is why we still join in singing that "we'll build a land (and a world) where we bind up the broken . . . where the captives go free." Let us make ourselves heard beyond our walls.

GLOBAL AND INTERFAITH CONNECTIONS

We would have every arbitrary barrier thrown down.
Margaret Fuller, no. 575

Dana Greeley, who was not often publicly critical of the denomination, complained in his reminiscences that the Overseas and Interfaith Relations Department was considered a very low priority, which seemed to him both tragic and "symptomatic of a pathetic provincialism." Of course such lack of support didn't stop him, and he described as "a gigantic achievement" how, despite concerns about the precarious financial situation, he got the 1963 General Assembly and the board to approve funding for this department. Authorization in hand, he and Max Gaebler, who had taken a leave of absence from his Madison, Wisconsin, pulpit to set up the department, started off for Asia and then Rome, where they attended the Second Vatican Council as observers from the International Association for Religious Freedom (IARF). It was there, as Greeley later recalled, that he sat within thirty feet of Pope John.

This was only the first of many overseas trips, and it was representative of the two tracks he, Gaebler, and later Homer Jack persisted in pushing the UUA's global connection: personal visits with religious leaders the world over, and enthusiastic support of IARF.

THE EVOLUTION OF IARF

The International Association for Religious Freedom had been established in 1900 at the annual meeting of the American Unitarian Association. Originally called the International Council of Unitarian and Other Liberal Religious Thinkers and Workers, its announced purpose was "to open communication with those in all lands who are striving to unite Pure Religion and Perfect Liberty." By 1907, the opening ceremony of its Congress included Protestant, Jewish, Muslim, Hindu, and Roman Catholic participants, as well as Unitarians, and Julia Ward Howe composed a hymn for the event. In 1930, the organization was renamed the International Association for Liberal Christianity and Religious Freedom, and in 1969 the reference to liberal Christianity was dropped. By this time, IARF meetings were attended by delegations from Japan, India, Latin America, and Africa, as well as Europe and North America. Describing itself as the oldest interfaith organization in the world, it now includes more than eighty faith groups.

Lean finances during the West administration precluded extensive international travel, but it was at Robert West's initiative that IARF was reorganized to make it more effective and to shore up its organizational structure. For the first time, its volunteer executive arrangement was replaced by a full-time professional executive, a UU minister born in Germany but trained in the United States. By this time there were member groups in twenty countries, including Rissho Kosei-kai, a highly successful liberal Japanese denomination based on a rational approach to Buddhism, as well as the Tsubaki Grand Shrine. In fact, RKK has become both an organizational and financial mainstay of the organization.

Eugene Pickett was able to resume the personal contacts of the Greeley years, and like Greeley he also demonstrated his strong link with IARF by taking on the IARF presidency after his UUA term expired. Another UUA leader who headed IARF was moderator Natalie Gulbrandsen. By Pickett's time, the number of member groups had grown to fifty-six, and in 1999, when the Association held its thirtieth World Congress, *IARF World* reported that more than 650 delegates and observers came from around the globe to discuss how their various religious traditions might contribute to the solution of the ecological crisis of our times.

There was, however, also a downside to the IARF's transformation into an increasingly multi-faith organization. The fairly conservative Swiss and Dutch members, especially, had not been too happy with the dropping of "Liberal Christianity" from the name, though they remained loyal and active; on the other hand, some North American Unitarian Universalists—while valuing the diversity of IARF—came to feel the need for an organization that focused more specifically on cross-border relations with Unitarians and Universalists in other lands. (Since consolidation affected only congregations in the United States and Canada, and Universalism had never spread much beyond this continent, this with few exceptions means other Unitarians.)

The lack of a strictly UU international body also caused one other problem: with IARF as our only international link, there was a tendency for North Amerian Unitarian Universalists to dominate it. It was symptomatic, President Buehrens believes, that we never managed to attract any non-Unitarian Universalists to the North American chapter of IARF. His hope when the International Council of Unitarian Universalists was eventually founded was that "by giving it away we can help IARF thrive, just as—instead of setting up the Red Cross as a denominational group—we were in on the creation of it, and then helped create a pluralistic, voluntary organization by letting it spin off."

THE EXTENDED FAMILY

David Usher was born in Australia, ministered to Unitarian and UU parishes in both England and the United States, and is now back in the UK, serving the Nazareth Unitarian Chapel in

Padiham, Lancashire. As such he almost personifies the international links of our faith, and in 1987 he made a motion at the British Unitarian General Assembly to start a conversation among the world's Unitarians and Universalists. The resolution passed, and in good volunteer organization tradition he was given the job of following up on his idea.

"It took eight years to bring the concept to fruition," he recalls. "Some were very indifferent to the idea and some were quite actively opposed." Among those not entirely enthusiastic was then-president William Schulz, who favored admitting overseas congregations into UUA membership. In fact, following his lead the board had in the 1980s voted to accept members from the Philippines, Pakistan, New Zealand, and Australia. Schulz also, though unsuccessfully, sought to launch a congregation in what was then the USSR. As Kay Montgomery, then as now UUA executive vice president, has pointed out, Schulz had an intense personal interest in our international relationships, doing an extensive amount of foreign traveling. Schulz, she says, "has a voracious appetite for other cultures. He wants to know what it's like to be an Inuit!"

Once John Buehrens became President in 1993, the policy changed. Buehrens appointed Kenneth MacLean, a retired minister, as his special assistant for international and interfaith relations. MacLean, significantly, had been the only member of the board to vote against the admission of foreign members, arguing that the UUA could not possibly provide the same services in Asia or Australia that it did to congregations at home and that its basic mission called for.

Following Buehrens's and MacLean's lead, the board now reversed itself and voted to admit no more international groups. Acting on the recommendation of Polly Guild, a retired UU minister and her husband, Ted, who were serving as volunteer international program coordinators, and Kenneth MacLean, who followed them, the UUA Board in 1995 voted to make funds available for a five-day conference in Essex, Massachusetts, that attracted delegates from sixteen countries. By the end of the five days, the International Council of Unitarians and Universalists had formally come into being. Its constitution begins, "We affirm our belief in religious community based upon liberty of conscience and of individual thought in matters of faith; the inherent worth and dignity of every person; justice and compassion in human relations; responsible stewardship of earth's living system; and our commitment to democratic principles." Usher was elected president; other officers came from the United States, Germany, Denmark, the United Kingdom, Canada, and Romania (i.e., Transylvania).

The organization sees its mission as providing an opportunity for Unitarian Universalists, Unitarians, and Universalists around the world to come together to share resources and inspiration. "We have held very successful leadership development conferences in South Asia and in Europe," Usher explains, "and we make every effort to do them in a way that does not suggest that we in the West know all the answers, but to come together as equals." Relations with IARF are amicable. "They are very understanding and supportive," according to Usher. "In fact they see ICUU as relieving them of some specifically in-house UU functions which are not appropriately theirs. I see the two organizations as making each other stronger."

Buehrens shares this view, seeing the redirection of our overseas initiative as "much less culturally imperialistic, as well as more effective in promoting international ties and relations. There has been a real increase in the overall global interaction of Unitarian Universalism." ICUU's third biennial meeting is scheduled for May of 2001 in Montreal, Quebec.

There are, of course, wide differences not only in economic circumstance among Unitarians and Universalists in various parts of the world, but also in theology. Nonetheless, Usher says "worship has been central in our meetings and conferences— very powerful and very unifying." Nor have these differences inhibited either the efforts to provide mutual support or the furtherance of common principles.

RECONNECTING WITH OUR ROOTS

Well represented in ICUU are the eighty thousand or so Unitarians in the Transylvanian section of Romania, who despite persecution, poverty, and isolation have maintained the faith inspired by Francis David that North American Unitarian Universalists also cherish as part of their heritage. Never was their suffering greater than in the twentieth century, when they were subjected successively to Hungarian fascism, Nazi domination, and the consequences of World War II when the Allies transferred the territory from Hungarian to Romanian control. Next there followed a Communist dictatorship that was hostile to all religion as well as determined to stamp out Transylvania's Hungarian language and ethnic identity. This effort went so far as to threaten to bulldoze the villages where most of the Unitarians lived so as to force the residents to move into more readily controllable towns. And, of course, it made contact with the West difficult, even dangerous.

But the link was never entirely broken. It goes back to 1825, when the Transylvanians sent congratulations to William Ellery Channing on the founding of the American Unitarian Association. When World War II broke out and the United States was still neutral, the Unitarian Service Committee tried to provide what help it could. After the war, North American Unitarian Universalists began to realize that not only did the Transylvanian Unitarians need our help in their struggle for sheer physical survival, but that we had much to learn from their example of courage and persistence. Unitarian Universalists who drop out because they are offended by one Sunday sermon might consider how they would bear up if their faith were challenged by the secret police of three successive tyrannies.

Among the first to reestablish the connection with Transylvanian Unitarians was Donald Szantho Harrington, for many years the senior minister of the UU Community Church in New York City. His middle name, Szantho, was the maiden name of his late first wife, Vilma, Unitarian by both birth and conviction and a graduate of the Unitarian seminary in Kolozsvar, capital of Transylvania. Harrington had met her when, newly graduated from Meadville/Lombard, he first visited Transylvania in 1938. They spent the first year of their married lives there, returning to the United States when war broke out in 1939.

After the war, it took the Harringtons until 1959 to get permission to return to what was now Romania, leading a tour that included Dana Greeley and Ernest Kuebler, president of IARF. "I shall never forget the first village we visited," Harrington reported in *Partner Church News*, "[We were] the first foreigners to be seen in Transylvania since before World War II. After an emotional service in the church, we returned to find our bus literally covered with flowers!" By the time Vilma died in 1982, the Harringtons had led six tours of fellow Unitarian Universalists and gained considerable insight into the lives of their Romanian co-religionists.

They discovered that there was a severe shortage of ministers since the Ceausescu dictatorship permitted only two or three students a year to enter the theological seminary. Some thirty to forty congregations had no clergy at all, and many of the remaining ministers were long past retirement age. Furthermore, not only was the government still centralized even after Ceausescu's downfall, but so were the Unitarians, with the bishop very much in charge. These Romanian Unitarian Bishops, by the way, used to serve for life, but that has now been cut to a six-year term.

Also, while people no longer disappear, Hungarians and Romanians are still not treated equally. For instance, Unitarian youth cannot attend high school unless they pass an exam in Romanian. Sheer economics also play a role in the population's sense of isolation. Some 90 percent live in villages that have changed little over the past four hundred years—farming communities ranging from 50 to 750 people, raising cows, hogs, sheep, chickens, geese, rabbits, sugar beets, and potatoes. Of course this stability also has a positive side: Some of the villages have churches that became Unitarian in the sixteenth century and have remained so ever since. As for the half dozen or so Unitarian churches on the Hungarian side of the border, while they are also struggling, at least they don't need to contend with ethnic prejudice.

When they realized the Unitarians' desperate need to restore their village churches or to build new ones in the cities, both

Harrington and Judit Gellerd, another UU with Transylvanian roots, turned to the Veatch program for help. Between 1991 and 1993, Veatch made available $160,000—some in matching grants—to be disbursed by the UUA. Gellerd also assumed a leading role in alerting Unitarian Universalists to the need to support their Eastern European co-religionists. And both Gellerd and the Harringtons came up with the same idea: appeal to North American congregations to "adopt" Transylvanian churches.

PARTNERS NOT PATRONS

As soon as Ceausescu was overthrown, UUA President William Schulz and Moderator Natalie Gulbrandsen led a UU delegation to find out first-hand how North Americans could help. After great difficulty in obtaining visas, they arrived in March of 1987. Despite the dictator's overthrow, Gulbrandsen discovered, not much had changed. "When I looked out the plane when we landed at Kolozsvar, there were guns aiming at us from every direction. It was not a very good welcome." Later—attesting to the continued efficiency of the secret police—when she mentioned to her husband in the privacy of their hotel room that she missed American toilet paper, some rolls were delivered the next day.

More to the point, it was an extremely emotional trip. "The people were so moved to see us," Gulbrandsen recalls. After one service at which she spoke, "as we were coming out of the church, they were waiting for us, just to touch us. And when we went to Torda [site of King Sigismund's diet], they said, 'We are very poor and we have no money for a gift for you, but we have something that is very dear to our hearts.' They had gone up high into the craggy mountains and had picked edelweiss to give to us. I still have it."

When she and Schulz returned home they conferred on how to provide meaningful help on a continuing and organized basis. While applauding the desire to adopt Transylvanian churches, and aware that in the 1920s as many as 112 U.S. congregations had successfully reached out to fellow churches overseas, they still felt that the current effort was too diffuse and uncoordinated. It needed structure. With the help of Gyorgy Andrasi, a Transylvanian who was taking courses at Meadville/Lombard, Gulbrandsen set about making a list of who was helping whom. "He knew his churches and I knew ours," she explains, "and we worked like beavers for a day-and-a-half identifying and notifying them. We said the program couldn't be effective if it continued to operate so informally, and though that made some people angry, we explained that there had to be coordination, and that it couldn't be done by random individuals making contact; that there had to be a vote by the congregation" to assure continuity and wide support.

The UUA then sent an invitation to all UUA congregations to apply to become sister (now called partner) churches, while Gellerd, through speeches and publications, continued to issue appeals to "Save Transylvanian Unitarianism." There was a flood of responses. Leon Hopper, then the minister in Golden, Colorado, was president of the UU Ministers' Association. As he recalls, the response "was like spontaneous combustion . . . an explosion of activity. Personal connections were forged [and] there were a remarkable number of visits to Transylvania that quickly resulted in deepened involvement and personal commitment."

But there was still not a clearly defined policy, and there was growing concern that the many uncoordinated visits by Westerners were putting an unfair burden on the endlessly hospitable but financially struggling Transylvanians. The UUMA decided to help. It set up a Transylvania ministers' support fund and Hopper went to Kolozsvar in March of 1993 to turn over the first $10,000. The local leaders decided to divide the money equally among all their clergy, and Hopper recalls his chagrin at what seemed to him a paltry sum per person. Aware of his embarrassment, someone turned to him and said, "Leon, that amount is the equivalent of a month's salary." Adds Hopper, "It was dawning upon me at a deep level of my being the hard reality of conditions and life in Transylvania."

At the 1993 General Assembly, a small group of those most concerned met to set up an organization that would promote the partnership program, act as a clearinghouse of information, and raise funds. They called it the UU Partner Church Council, with Hopper as president. In his first statement to the group he said, "Our . . . initial response for support was charged with emotion and a bit of nostalgia. It is now important for us to be grounded in recognition of the profound integrity and courage of our partner colleagues. We need to remember that we are engaged in a *partner* relationship. Healthy partnerships exact a practice of both giving and receiving." Or as Sandor Kovacs, a Transylvanian minister, so tactfully put it on a visit to the United States, "As in all relationships, ours needs to be built upon equality and mutual respect. It is not for us to attempt to impose our vision or our will upon the life of your church, any more than you would presume to do so with us."

Reflecting on the spirit of partnership, Leon Hopper quotes Albert Schweitzer (some of whose books were published by Beacon Press and who late in life joined the Church of the Larger Fellowship): "At times our own light goes out and is rekindled by a spark from another person. Each of us has cause to think with deep gratitude of those who have lit the flame within." In many a North American UU congregation, that flame has been lit by their Eastern European partner church. As of the start of 2000, the number of partner congregations totaled at least 160 in Canada and the United States, and some 224 in Romania, Hungary, and the Czech Republic. Now the Partnership Church Council is considering how the model might be applied not only in Poland but in the Philippines and India.

According to John Gibbons, parish minister in Bedford, Massachusetts, and current council president, hundreds of Unitarian Universalists have by now visited Transylvania, and well over a million dollars has gone to the denomination's European partners. Unitarians in Romania, he adds, still feel very much like an endangered minority as the government persists in trying to move ethnic Romanians into Hungarian-language areas. To be fair to all sides, however, it's important to realize the multi-ethnic history of this area, and that for much of the time it was the Romanians who felt oppressed. After a brief period during the seventeenth century of what the *Columbia Encyclopedia* calls Transylvania's golden age, when it was "the only European country where Roman Catholics, Calvinists, Lutherans, and Unitarians lived in mutual tolerance," it came successively under Ottoman then Austrian (later Austro-Hungarian) control, became Romanian at the end of World War I, was annexed by Hungary during World War II, then reverted to Romania when the war ended. There was only one constant: Regardless of who was in charge, after the brief reign of King John Sigismund, tolerance was never restored.

Summing up the transatlantic link, Gibbons says, "The Transylvanians have given North Americans the gift of awareness of our religious roots. The connection has really had a transforming effect on our congregations, giving them a fresh appreciation of our history and of our Christian heritage. As many of our humanist congregations have been challenged by the proud liberal Christianity of Eastern Europe, it has engendered a new respect for the diversity of our religious heritage."

Gibbons is especially impressed by the impact trips to Transylvania have had on UU teenagers. "When they stand in the pulpit where Francis David stood and hold the communion ware that David held, that experience of touching their own history has a profound effect." These are not pen pal relationships, he stresses, though they might start that way. "These are bonding experiences for mutual enrichment."

The material benefits that have enriched the people of Transylvania include the farm equipment acquired by the villages, the cooperatives they have begun to form, the young people brought to the United States to study modern farming techniques, the credit that has paid for a flour mill and bakery, and the English teacher at the theological institute in Kolozsvar supported by Meadville/Lombard. More subtly, they have acquired the gift of hope and a sense of connection with a larger world after many years of isolation. Another link is that each year Starr King School opens a scholarship to a student from Transylvania.

The cumulative result is that our European co-religionists may be developing a new attitude toward women, and a less hierarchical relationship among their churches.

Max Gaebler has observed that the partnership initiative is the strongest grass-roots movement among Unitarian Universalists since civil rights caught our imagination. John Buehrens adds that the connection is teaching us about diversity and "otherness" in a way that reinforces our domestic work of anti-racism. For all these reasons, though the Partnership Church Council is an independent organization, it receives administrative support from the UUA through the Office of International Relations.

THE UUA AS NEXUS

The Office of International Relations connects the UUA not only with the Partnership Church Council but with all our related multinational organizations—IARF, ICUU, and the World Conference on Religion and Peace (WCRP). This latter body, inspired by Dana Greeley and Nikkyo Niwano of Japan, was initiated at a six-day conference in Kyoto in October 1970. Homer Jack, who served for many years as its secretary general, recalls in his autobiography that "several hundred religious leaders, from a wide range of religions and nationalities, assembled for the express purpose of discussing the relation between religion and peace." The greatest achievement, he reflected, "was that the conference was held—and successfully." His sense of achievement was indeed justified considering that the conference took place against the background of the Vietnam war, and the closing statement included expressions of concern not only about that conflict, but also about the arms race, racial intolerance, and the suffering of the poor.

The most recent meeting of WCRP was held in Amman, Jordan, in November of 1999, and was attended by John Buehrens, Olivia Holmes—who followed MacLean as head of the international relations office—and Rob Cavenaugh of the UUA Washington Faith in Action office. They were joined by fifteen hundred religious leaders from sixty countries, and heard talks by the president of Indonesia and the king of Jordan. Buehrens, who chaired the business sessions, has called WCRP "the most effective and significant international interfaith organization," crediting it with bringing together rival religious leaders in an attempt to end the fighting in such killing fields as Sierra Leone and Bosnia.

The international congress meets every five years, and both Buehrens and MacLean also attended the previous meeting in Italy in 1994. Demonstrating the active participation of the world's major faiths, the meeting began in the Vatican and, as MacLean recalls, was attended by about one thousand religious leaders "wearing every kind of regalia and symbol you can imagine."

Unitarian Universalists were also well represented at the third Parliament of the World's Religions in Cape Town, South Africa, in 1999, following a tradition established at the first such parliament in 1893. Furthermore, President Buehrens was one of roughly eight hundred religious leaders plus one thousand other participants who joined in the Millennium World Peace Summit of Religious and Spiritual Leaders in August of 2000. The conference opened at the United Nations with an address by Secretary General Kofi Annan, who acknowledged, "Religion is frequently equated with light, but we all know the practice of religion can have its dark side. Religious extremism has too often repressed women and minorities. Religion has often stoked conflict, and religious leaders have not always spoken out." Among the religions represented at the summit, according to the organizers' final report, were Ba'hai, Buddhism, Christianity, Confucianism, Hinduism, Indigenous Peoples, Islam, Jainism, Judaism, Shinto, Sikhism, Taoism, and Zoroastrianism. Unitarian Universalism wasn't listed separately (on the international scene we're often classified according to our liberal Christian roots), but our commitments to the pursuit of peace, to "each person's inherent dignity," to nonviolence, to freedom of religion, and to "care for the earth's ecological systems" were eloquently echoed in the final declaration signed by the participants. The statement concluded, "We appeal to the followers of all religious traditions and to the human community as a whole to cooperate in building peaceful societies, to seek mutual understanding through dialogue . . . , to refrain from violence, to practice compassion, and to uphold the dignity of all life." It is in the pursuit of such ideals that the UUA has, since its founding, put great stress on interfaith activities as one more way to make real our sixth Principle: "to affirm and promote the goal of world community with peace, liberty, and justice for all."

SUPPORTING THE UNITED NATIONS

It is also dedication to the goal of international cooperation and world peace that has kept UU volunteers working hard over the years to maintain the Unitarian Universalist United Nations Office, an associate member organization of the UUA, with an office located in New York City across from UN headquarters. Relying for funding on individual and congregational support, as well as grants, it has enlisted more than four hundred volunteer "envoys" in UU congregations who inform their fellow members of news and action opportunities, promote UN Sunday observances, and in general foster support for the United Nations. They take as their inspiration the words of Adlai Stevenson, twice candidate for the presidency, ambassador to the UN from 1961 to 1965, and himself a Unitarian Universalist, who declared, "I believe the cause of freedom and peace has a glorious future in the world. And in that future the United Nations will play a mighty part." The UN Office president is Benjamin Bortin, minister of the Unitarian Church of Staten Island.

ALL THE MONEY IN THE WORLD

In terms of individual lives, of human dignity and human rights, the one activity of the Office of International Relations with the greatest impact is undoubtedly the non-sectarian Holdeen India Program. Along with the oil and gas wealth of the UU Congregation at Shelter Rock that has undergirded our denomination, this is a story that tempts one to believe in a benign providence looking out for Unitarian Universalists.

Once upon a time (it sounds like a fairy tale, so we might as well tell it like one), there was a rich man in New York by the name of Jonathan Holdeen. He took to heart a conceit developed by Benjamin Franklin: that if you took a few pennies, let them earn interest and made at most modest withdrawals, sooner or later you (or more likely your descendants) would accumulate all the money in the world. That sounded to Holdeen like a good idea, so he went about setting up a number of trust funds, naming as proximate beneficiary the American Unitarian Association, with Franklin's state of Pennsylvania to receive the amount accumulated at the end of five hundred or one thousand years.

Next came the intervention not of a fairy godmother but of UU lawyers who found out that the money that was supposed to go to what was by then the UUA was being diverted by the trustees. They initiated a series of court cases that seemed to go on for as long as Sleeping Beauty's nap but eventually led to the establishment of trusts that are independent of the UUA. Some are for "maternal and child welfare" in India; one allows expenditures throughout Asia; and still another allows the UUA to name other charities to receive the income. This last trust benefits the Liberal Religious Charitable Society, a support organization for the UUA, and makes contributions to such international organizations as IARF, ICUU, WCRP, and the Partner Church Council.

The India trusts support the UU Holdeen India Program. These trusts specify that the money be used to improve the lives of the poor in India, with emphasis on women. The program has been a trailblazer in effecting social change, working with the poorest of the poor—with bonded laborers and *dalits,* the people who used to be called untouchables. With grants of some $700,000 a year, the program supports the work of about thirty organizations in five Indian states; their basic common purpose is to help oppressed people to organize for human rights and social change, using women's leadership.

The program is administered by a director, Katharine Sreedhar, who works out of Washington, DC. She puts great emphasis on leadership training, to provide not just temporary amelioration but to create effective social change. With this goal in mind, she makes every effort not to stop with providing a grant but to find ways to strengthen the structure of the beneficiary organization. MacLean, who worked closely with Sreedhar while at UUA headquarters, cites these examples. "Maybe they need an office to conduct their business. Maybe they need a jeep to get around. Maybe they need to provide health care or to increase salaries to attract and keep good staff members." To provide this sort of help, Sreedhar spends a good part of her time in India, and MacLean himself paid repeated visits.

Sreedhar reports that in support of its objectives the program seeks out Indian partners with a demonstrated ability to reach and organize the most disadvantaged so as to promote democratic governance, people's initiatives, and women's full leadership and participation. By now there are thirty such partners —there has been a total of fifty-nine to date—and they have succeeded in building cadres of confident leaders, expanding their bargaining power, and acquiring technical and management expertise—even to influence public policy. They have organized unions, set up cooperatives and women's self-help and savings and credit groups, developed new employment opportunities. Increasingly, they have taken on controversial, risky issues, such as campaigns for tribal land, water and forest rights, minimum wages, and campaigns against gender and communal violence. Even when they grow to the point where they no longer require outside funding, the Holdeen program often continues to provide support by helping to forge alliances and providing consulting services.

In order to extend its effectiveness, the Holdeen program also tries to build networks with other organizations and government agencies with parallel objectives, and seeks to secure additional financial support for its Indian partners from other donors. As Kenneth MacLean said in his final report, "The Unitarian Universalist Holdeen India Program is one of the most significant activities of this whole denomination in terms of its impact on individual lives."

THE ASIAN UNITARIANS

No one would question the value of such non-sectarian help but, some might ask, are there not also Unitarians in India and how are we helping them?

The answer is that there have been Unitarians in the Khasi Hills since the 1880s, when a young man named Hajom Kissor Singh converted to Christianity, developed doubts, met a Unitarian minister, and decided he was a Unitarian, too. The bond was strengthened in the 1930s, when Margaret Barr, an English Unitarian, decided to live in the Khasi Hills and sought to provide health care and education; in fact, the British Unitarians still support a health center at Khariang. Today, the Unitarian Union of North East India (just north of Bangladesh) consists of thirty-two churches and six fellowships, with a total of some nine thousand members and a school supported by each of the churches. The UUA, through the Holdeen Asia Fund, offers grants of about $30,000 a year and is helping to finish the building of a high school.

More fundamentally, the UUA is seeking to achieve a partnership based on equality and mutual respect, one that avoids dominance or dependence, and in furtherance of that goal it assigned a UU minister, John Rex, for a six-month period, to study the language, conduct services, and make himself available for training ministers, teachers, and lay leaders. The objective, says Kenneth MacLean, was to "enable us to have more confidence that the resources we provide are filling the needs the people really feel, not just what they think we want to provide." To further deepen our understanding of their culture and their distinctive brand of non-Christian Unitarianism, MacLean himself paid several visits, as have John Buehrens and Denise Davidoff. To quote MacLean once more, "Such relationships across such a great cultural divide are not developed overnight. Our efforts will take time to give us the confidence that together we know what we are doing to improve the lives of the people of the Unitarian communities in the Khasi Hills, and that we are truly working together."

A similar program is under way in the Philippines. Again a UU minister, Frederic Muir of the UU Church of Annapolis, Maryland, spent six months not just to help the sixteen member societies of the Unitarian Universalist Church in the Philippines, but to build a partnership based on a better understanding of their culture, their lives, their religion, and their needs. Their needs, he found, are very similar to those of the people in India, though they are perhaps less isolated, not only geographically, but also because their minister and denominational president, Rebecca Quimada-Sienes, the daughter of the Church's founder, holds a degree from Meadville/Lombard and was ordained in the United States. Like Rex, Muir had the unusual qualification of having been in similar settings before.

There are also small related groups in Lahore, Pakistan, and in Sri Lanka, but whatever the location, the hope is not to act as missionaries, or to tell people what we think they should do. The hope is to help them find their own ways to develop, to foster and train their own leadership, and to determine what their goals are and how to achieve them. It is the mission of the Office of International Relations—acting on behalf of all Unitarian Universalists—to aid them in developing their spiritual lives and at the same time tackle the problems arising from their poverty and lack of resources.

That aspiration isn't limited to a single office or program. Another hymn UU congregations often join in singing is "Our world is one world." They know, of course, that this is an ideal, not a geopolitical fact. Nor, even if we could, do we wish to make this a Unitarian Universalist world. What we do wish for—fervently— is a world where our ideals and aspirations will take root and flourish so that some day no one will be killed or starved or tortured because of their nationality, their race, their faith, their opinions, their sexual orientation, or the way they choose to live. Then, indeed, there will be one world in which everyone can feel at home.

THE PROMISE

A Faith for the Future

If, recognizing the interdependence of all life, we strive to build community, the strength we gather will be our salvation.

Marjorie Bowens-Wheatley, no. 576

Was the combining of the Universalist Church of America and the American Unitarian Association a success? Has it met the expectations of those who for many decades dreamed of it and of those many others who worked with so much hope and enthusiasm to bring it to fruition?

The predictions that we would soon double our membership have, the record shows, not been realized, at least not yet. Neither, except perhaps metaphorically, have the high hopes typified by Donald Harrington's sermon celebrating the launch of the Unitarian Universalist Association at Boston's Symphony Hall, when he proclaimed that ours was to be "a new world faith."

Does that mean the skeptics were right?

No one person can provide the answer. That is why, in conducting the interviews that (together with published recollections and official records) form the core of this book, everyone with personal knowledge of consolidation or its aftermath was asked to assess its results. The answers form not so much a consensus as a mosaic of dominant themes. Here are three that stand out, juxtaposed with some representative quotations.

The main motive for consolidation—to join two religious traditions that had so much in common into a single religious family—has worked better than expected. No one nowadays asks, "Are you a Unitarian or a Universalist?" Instead there is a sense of common identity, and the denomination that took shape is far more than the sum of its original components. Says Gordon McKeeman, "When I visited congregations as a candidate for the UUA presidency, I was amazed at how homogenous we are. You can go from one end of this continent to the other and Unitarian Universalists are immediately recognizable. The real benefit of merger was theological and spiritual enrichment."

Consolidation was inevitable. Without it, the Universalist tradition might not have survived, with many congregations disappearing and others joining more conservative denominations. However, the Unitarians also benefited. "The Universalists would not have survived," says Leon Hopper, while "the money from various Universalist conventions sustained the UUA through some very difficult periods." Jack Mendelsohn puts it this way: "Merger was tremendously successful in terms of creating resources for strengthening congregations and supporting new congregations." Not realized, however, "was our hope that with combined resources we could do better in influencing public policy."

Universalism won. Though the Universalists were the weaker partner at the beginning, Universalism "won" in the long run— not in the sense of power, but because Unitarian Universalist values today are closer to historic Universalism than of Unitarianism. One of those sharing this opinion is Kay Montgomery. "I think the Universalists won," she says. "It's been very healthy to have the Universalist tradition to refer to as people try to figure out how to live in this complex and secular age." David Pohl agrees. "Merger was an affair of the heart more than anything else and overall I think it worked. Especially in recent years, there has been a very conscious effort to recover the Universalist emphasis on a more egalitarian faith, one that emphasizes feeling as well as reason, one that attempts to be less 'classist,' less elitist." Or as Ernest Cassara puts it, "All that was lost was snob appeal," though Charles Gaines feels that we also lost the Universalists' evangelism and populism.

One conclusion that seems beyond challenge is that the first forty years of the UUA have seen great changes in what we believe and how we perceive ourselves—not a total transformation, of course, but an evolution that could not have been anticipated by either the supporters or opponents of consolidation. At the same time, there have also been some surprising constants, not least in our demographic descriptors.

WHO WE ARE

A readership study on behalf of *UUWorld* magazine in 1978 (the earliest such data on record) showed that one in three of the respondents had high incomes, that 75 percent were college graduates while 40 percent held an advanced degree. Half were over fifty, and 44 percent classified themselves as being in a professional occupation.

Not quite ten years later, in 1987, another survey showed little change. Though the questions were not asked in precisely the same way, such data as are comparable are strikingly similar. More than three-quarters of the respondents considered themselves either middle or upper-middle class, and a similar percentage had college degrees or had done at least some graduate work. The majority again worked in professional, technical, or managerial jobs, and the median age was in the high fifties. Other tidbits: three-fourths considered themselves either somewhat or very liberal in their political outlook, and 40 percent each—for a total of four out of five—lived in either a city or a suburb.

Another decade passed, and in 1996 the *World* once again profiled its readers. This time their mean income (now that the dollar figures are comparable to today's) was $63,900, with 13 percent reporting incomes in excess of $100,000. No great change, either, in educational attainment: 23 percent had "only" college degrees while a whopping 47 percent had graduate degrees; an additional 15 percent had done some graduate study. The median age was fifty-three, while 49 percent were in either professional or managerial positions. Finally, 96 percent (a question not asked before) described their ethnic background as "white." The consistent favorite leisure activity was reading books, with public TV and radio ranking at or near the top of causes (other than the church) to which Unitarian Universalists contributed.

THE ISSUES THAT PERSIST

Another constant, along with the demographics, is that almost all the issues that proved most troublesome at the time of consolidation are still with us. Several concern aspects of governance, and while they are not nearly as hotly debated now as they were then, they still bubble up often enough to indicate that they have not gone away.

One lively initial debate centered on the role of the UUA's president: whether he (as everyone then took for granted) should be elected by the General Assembly and combine both ceremonial and executive functions, or whether the new association would be better off with the Universalist pattern of a purely ceremonial head plus a full-time CEO, both appointed by the Board. While the question was resolved in favor of a strong AUA-type president, this didn't make the issue go away. It was addressed once more in 1976 by a special committee of the Board, and yet again in 1993 by a Commission on Governance. Both opted for a Board-appointed executive director, but each time the General Assembly stuck with the status quo.

Still the question keeps being raised, especially in election years, when candidates for the presidency spend considerable time and money campaigning. Of course, such campaigning also gives a large number of local congregants the opportunity to meet the future president. William Schulz estimates that when he ran against Sandra Caron in 1985 they appeared at more than three hundred of the roughly one thousand congregations. And Schulz also defines the role of president in terms that neither a ceremonial head nor a staff administrator could easily fill. The president, he believes, should be "a spokesperson in the larger culture . . .

someone who can articulate the UU faith and philosophy in a way that catches the imagination of the larger world."

A related question is whether the moderator should be elected by the GA or whether the UUA board should pick its own presiding officer. Twice in our history, in the Greeley/Dimmock years and again when Sandra Caron was moderator while Eugene Pickett was president, rivalry between these two officers proved divisive and disruptive. On the other hand, when the two officers work well together, as West did with Fisher and Schulz with Gulbrandsen, it makes for a strong partnership. President Buehrens credits his constructive relationship with Moderator Davidoff for moving the denomination toward the center and, due to his Christian and her Jewish backgrounds, for providing greater emphasis on interfaith activities. Also, Davidoff has concentrated during her two terms on visiting congregations, thus doubling the opportunities for members everywhere to have a first-hand encounter with a denominational leader. Kay Montgomery, from her perspective as a senior staff member under three presidents, adds that the close working relationship of Davidoff and Buehrens has led to easier relations not only with the Board but also with and among the staff. In any case, GA delegates have consistently voted against all proposals to change the moderator's role.

They have also rejected recurrent suggestions that the assembly itself should meet only every other year. Quite clearly, those attending GAs like things as they are. But are these delegates truly representative? Should there be absentee ballots for congregations that can't afford to be represented, as there are for elections of officers? What about electronic "real-time" voting? Moderator Davidoff has heard many such suggestions and complaints, and her standard reply is, "It's *your* GA. If you don't like it, change it." So far, her challenge has gone unmet.

DECENTRALIZATION

The longest-running issue, however, concerns the balance of power. Many Universalists before merger bemoaned the fact that their denominational structure was too weak; Unitarian critics, meanwhile, accused strong presidents such as Frederick May Eliot and Dana Greeley of gathering too much power at what critics tend to call "Boston" or "25." This source of tension takes two forms. One is whether congregational polity is being eroded; the other concerns the proper role of districts.

The debate about congregational polity will never be settled since there is an inherent ambivalence in our structure that goes back to the days of the New England Puritans. What it boils down to is that, yes, congregations are self-governing but, no, they are not self-sufficient, and to the extent that anyone asks for parental help or joins in a cooperative movement, she, he, or it surrenders some measure of sovereignty. That this can lead to friction was demonstrated in the United States by the long controversies about states' rights, culminating but not ending in a bloody Civil War; in Europe the issue is being replayed by the members of the European Union; in the UUA it enlivens the pages of *UU Voice*, an independent tabloid publication that tends to take a contrarian view of denominational affairs. It's a debate that is not likely ever to end, but as long as both the critics of UUA policies and those asking for more and better services keep pushing the pendulum from opposite ends, it will presumably wind up somewhere in a reasonable middle.

The proper role of intermediate organizations was another flashpoint of disagreement when the structure of the UUA was being hammered out. Significantly, Gordon McKeeman recalls that long after the other committees preparing for consolidation had completed their work, "the committee on regional organization was still hassling." The compromise that emerged called for districts that are far less autonomous than either the Universalist state assemblies or the Unitarian conferences. For one thing, most don't have their own money. For another, while they elect their own boards which, in turn, appoint the district executive, the choices are made from a panel submitted by headquarters.

But soon after consolidation came the greatest shift in the balance of power in our history: the election of district trustees. Today, all but four members-at-large of the UUA Board are chosen by the districts. As if to confound his critics, it was a reform strongly supported by Dana Greeley and, quite obviously, enthusiastically endorsed by the first batch of district leaders. Not that everyone has been happy with that system. Some felt (and still feel today) that that there is a danger that those elected to the board have a parochial rather than continental perspective, leading to conflicts with the president, and that, because they may have been factional candidates, they push the "cause of the moment." Others point out that nominating committees do a better job of making the board representative not only geographically but also by gender, race, age, and sexual orientation. They are also more likely to recruit people with national reputations—and deep pockets.

Worse, the critics go on, since participation in district affairs is often sparse and sporadic, district trustees may not be truly representative of their congregations, though William Sinkford, head of the department that works with districts, believes this situation is improving. He admits that many districts used to be "more virtual than real," with very poorly attended annual meetings, but now, he says, with the help of consultants who have been trained by either the district executive or UUA staff, "they are moving out of adolescence into adulthood." Their committee structure is functioning better, he adds, and "they take their organizational tasks very seriously."

Meanwhile, the Buehrens administration has made extensive efforts to decentralize UUA operation. There are now district programs as well as religious education consultants; the Young Adult/Campus Ministry office is in Princeton, New Jersey, while the Holdeen India Fund is administered from Washington, DC. Altogether, there are forty-five regular full- or part-time UUA employees who do not work in Boston, out of a total (depending on vacancies) of roughly 210—a little over 20 percent.

Also worthy of mention is the President's Council, which brings together some of the "heavy hitters" (not only in terms of money but also of prestige and influence) who tend not to get elected to the board. They are advice givers, says Montgomery, picked to help the stewardship of the association, and though mindful that they are not meant to run things, they have been remarkably effective in bringing an additional perspective to the UUA's policies and operations.

THE CHANGES IN WHAT WE BELIEVE

The one area where the most significant change has taken place is in the dominant emphases of Unitarian Universalist theology. And no wonder: Like a flowing river, we are (despite the demographic consistency) not the same people. As various contributors to Scott Alexander's book *Salted with Fire* point out, an estimated 85 to 90 percent of Unitarian Universalists today were not raised in our faith. What's more, the turnover continues. Ralph Mero estimates that of one hundred new members who join an average congregation, some eighty are gone within one or two years. What's significant is that these new members come for motives quite different from those that inspired new recruits forty years ago.

Back then, the bulk of those who joined were "come-outers"— people who had turned their backs on the religion they were raised in. They tended to be distrustful of authority and of anything that reminded them of the faiths they had discarded. In 1963, the authors of *The Free Church in a Changing World*, compiling the reports of six commissions appointed to define the "true task" of the new denomination, found it necessary to defend the use of the word "theology," and to argue that a "sermon should not be a block of analytical discourse."

As that admonition suggests, humanism was a powerful strain in the new denomination, and whoever wasn't a humanist tended to be a theist. Indeed, "Are you a humanist or a theist?" was by no means an unusual question when two Unitarian Universalists first encountered each other. To put it more broadly, the split was between those who believed that there is some purpose, some direction to the universe, and those who assumed that whatever purpose there is to life has to be defined by man (as they said in those days) the meaning maker. In fact, that was the title of a popular RE curriculum, which, incidentally, never once mentioned Unitarian Universalism! Arvid Straub reports in the Alexander book that in the early 1980s, when search committees were asked to list what their congregations were looking for in a sermon, "intellectual stimulation" was the top criterion, and many sermons were, in fact, almost indistinguishable from lectures or book reviews. At the opposite end of the spectrum, some UU Christian congregations continued (and continue today) to celebrate communion services.

Those sharp divisions have been eased. There are still strict humanists who cling to the premise that "if you can't prove it empirically it has no meaning." There are still Christian Unitarian Universalists. But there are also Buddhist, Hindu, Jewish, pagan, earth-centered, and Goddess-worshipping Unitarian Universalists. The broad middle ground is occupied by those who might best be described as "non-orthodox humanists." Without denying the primacy of reason, they also attach great importance to spiritual values. They accept the role of ritual and emotion in worship services, and in some cases are even willing to experiment with healing and prayer services. In any case, as Rebecca Parker points out, the tension between humanism and spirituality is being resolved as people realize that they are not as much at odds as once was thought.

Which brings us back to the expectation of those who have been joining our congregations for at least the past ten years. To quote Barry Andrews in the Alexander book, today's newcomers are likely to be motivated "by a strong if inarticulate desire to address a religious void in their lives. . . . They are looking for a 'spiritual experience' and for a community that cares about them and shares their values." Hence they tend to be more comfortable with religious language and ritual than the come-outers of previous years.

As for today's sermons, according to Suzanne P. Meyers, another minister who contributed to *Salted with Fire*, only members born before 1947 still prefer emotionally neutral sermons that deal with ideas and issues. Admitting that it may be a bit of an overgeneralization, she goes on to say that among baby boomers, "celebration and spiritual renewal is number one. . . .

198/ OUR WIDER HORIZONS

They prefer sermons that deal with feelings, personal dilemmas, life passages and spiritual growth," and often look for help in personal crises.

The turning point in the religious emphasis in the denomination came gradually, unobtrusively. But if a single date can be assigned to the watershed it was William Schulz's sermon at the 1986 General Assembly. He used language that none of his predecessors—not the theist Greeley nor the humanists West and Pickett—would ever have chosen. "Reason is still a cherished standard in our religious repertoire," he declared, "but reason is coming to be supplemented by our immediate apprehension of the Holy and by our conviction that the Holy is embodied in the abundance of a scarred Creation." He chose those capital letters when he published his sermon in *Finding Time.*

He went on to trace the rediscovery of spirituality to "a greater valuing of women's experience, a new openness . . . to Eastern faith and practice; and of course a growing disillusionment with materialism." Proclaiming himself to be still a humanist, he nonetheless said that "the simple liberalism of my childhood— the faith that if we protect fundamental civil liberties, if everyone is given a platform and a voice, we will end up with a civil community—suddenly appeared inadequate to the realities of war and iniquity. . . . We needed a compelling vision of the ends toward which we struggled."

His use of the word *rediscovery* is apt. As has often been pointed out, these beliefs in many ways mirror nineteenth-century Transcendentalism—the Emersonian concept of the oversoul and the Thoreauvian desire to live deliberately and "suck out all the marrow of life." Or, if you prefer, we have rediscovered the essence of Universalism.

Spirituality is now so widely invoked in UU circles that some, like Eugene Pickett, suspect it of being a buzz word. Historian Ernest Cassara says that the emphasis on spirituality bothers him. "It's some vague and amorphous idea," he says, "but never defined," and Natalie Gulbrandsen states bluntly that spirituality is a fad. Jack Mendelsohn sees both value and risk. He is concerned that the emphasis on spirituality can be "slick and ambiguous," with the result that "young ministers today are not on fire to influence public policy, to shape a better society. Instead, their business is spirituality, prayer, healing, meditation, community." Those are all useful, he concludes, "but only if used instrumentally for some higher, more challenging objective, such as a better society."

These are, however, likely to be minority opinions, perhaps reflecting a generational split. The majority of Unitarian Universalists probably agree with Paul Johnson that the emphasis on spirituality is "an acknowledgement of the mystery of existence."

WHAT BINDS US TOGETHER

Again, let's put some statistical flesh on these bones of generalizations by comparing two opinion surveys.

In 1967, a report on a survey of beliefs conducted by a Committee on Goals appointed by the UUA board revealed that only 10.6 percent of respondents were born either Universalists or Unitarians. Only 2.9 percent believed in God as a supernatural being, as against 28 percent who saw God as "an irrelevant concept," though 44.2 percent agreed that "'God' may be appropriately used as a name for some natural processes within the universe, such as love or creative evolution." Fifty-seven percent would not define their religion as Christian; 52 percent thought of Unitarian Universalism as "a distinctive humanistic religion."

Then, at the 1998 General Assembly in Rochester, New York, Clark Olsen, an ordained UU minister and consultant on strategic planning, reported on an analysis of more than eight thousand survey forms returned by readers of *UU World*. The respondents identified themselves as humanists (61 percent), earth or nature centered (19 percent), theists (13 percent), Christians (9.5 percent), and mystics (6.7 percent), with scattered "votes" for Buddhism and Judaism. Despite this diversity, an amazing 52 percent, when asked "What is the 'glue' that binds individual UUs and congregations together?" replied, "Shared values and principles," while 42.5 percent chose "Acceptance, respect, and support for each other as individuals." What's significant about these results is that these two values were either the first or second choice of every one of the theological groups. Commenting on the survey results, William Sinkford said, "Although we struggle with it, there is a center to Unitarian Universalism. Although there are differences, the consistency and coherence is really stunning." To which John Buehrens added that the responses to question after question showed "a very strong commitment to becoming more diverse—culturally, racially—and to promote these values in our communities and in the larger world." Indeed, an overwhelming 63 percent when asked "What are your dreams for the UU movement?" chose as their answer "Become a visible and influential force for good in the world."

If, as this survey suggests, a majority of Unitarian Universalists believes that what unites us are shared values and principles, that still leaves open the question as to what those values are. Since they were adopted with only one dissenting vote and have found wide acceptance ever since, the UUA Principles and Purposes presumably provide the answer. But Walter Royal Jones, the person most closely identified with their development, asks a searching question: faced with a heart operation, with great grief or great stress, what do we have to fall back on? Is it likely that many of us would, on our death bed, ask to have the Principles and Purposes read to us for solace and support? Nor are we likely to find help in the current denominational emphasis on diversity, as summed up on the front of the order of service of the First Unitarian Church of Oakland, California, that "We are an intentionally diverse community." Yet obviously there is *something* that holds us together, something beyond a common (but often neglected) history, something more than the strength we find in community, something that provides the rationale for valuing diversity and for affirming our principles.

Of the fact that there is such a "something" there can be no doubt. Not only present-day Unitarian Universalists but the members of both predecessor denominations have been distrustful of institutions, yet the UUA and its member congregations persist and thrive. Another characteristic of Unitarian Universalists is that for at least two centuries we have vigorously disagreed about beliefs, yet without certain tacit assumptions we would not have bothered to argue.

So then what is the glue that holds us together?

Perhaps we can find a clue in the way we conduct memorial services. Several ministers, both in print and in conversation, have observed that memorial services are the one religious exercise we do best. Jane Rzepka, minister of the Church of the Larger Fellowship, said recently about a service for her father, "I was relieved and pleased that . . . mainstream Unitarian Universalism felt so utterly satisfying to us in the face of death." Even more telling, many of us have had the experience of non-UU guests turning to us at the end of such a service to say that it was one of the most moving religious observances they had ever attended. Why?

It can't be simply because we routinely say that we have come together not to mourn but to celebrate a life. That is a common theme in many denominations. Nor that we let relatives and friends share their remembrances, with humor if they can, or with straightforward reminiscence or sentiment if they prefer. That, too, is not unique to Unitarian Universalists. What, then, makes the difference?

It may well be not anything we do, but what we *don't* do.

We don't offer false comfort with promises of reunion in a hereafter. We don't recite rote prayers or follow empty rituals. What we do, instead, is to strive, above all, to be honest—honest about the person we are commemorating, honest about our grief and our sense of loss, honest about our confusion in the face of death, honest about our yearning, in the words of Saul Bellow, "to know what we are and what we are for, to know our purpose, to seek grace," without claiming to have a monopoly on the answers.

And therein may lie the irreducible core that remains after all the temporal fashions in terminology and practice are stripped away: our adamant refusal to believe—or pretend to believe—anything our reason, our experience, our communal search for truth tells us is not believable. As so often, Ralph Waldo Emerson said it best, "All that is clear today is not to lie."

What sets us apart from those who claim to be indifferent to religion is that we want answers. What sets us apart from virtually every other faith is that we will not accept *easy* answers. That holds true whether we call ourselves humanists or theists, agnostics or atheists, pagans or mystics; it holds true for the certain and the uncertain, for those who put primacy on intuition or on the intellect or give equal attention to both. From time to time we may even change our minds, but one thing is forever clear to us if religion is to be taken seriously: it is necessary not to lie. From that fierce commitment flow the values that we cling to, and from which, in turn, comes our devotion to Unitarian Universalism.

EPILOGUE

At the threshold of a new millennium, as the UUA enters its sixth decade, let us consider not only what has gone before but what is likely to lie ahead.

The two people who are in the best position to take stock— having for eight years witnessed at first hand the achievements, challenges, and commitments of hundreds of our congregations and thousands of their members—are our moderator and our president.

Says Denise Davidoff, "I have a great sense of encouragement. Our congregations are vibrant and full of energy, filled with people in their twenties and thirties. Our RE classes are bursting. There is a 65-percent increase in local fundraising, and there is a surge of good feeling."

John Buehrens is equally hopeful. "During my presidency I have participated in the dedication of 106 new church buildings, and many of our congregations are moving back to the center of town."

An increased emphasis on global and interfaith activities is another positive sign. Buehrens notes,

> There are three times as many youth groups as there were in 1994; there is a remarkable increase in generosity; and we are enjoying robust organizational health. Many of our smaller churches still need more funds for extension and we need to start more churches. And, yes, the impact of the culture presents the risk of what I call 'internal consumerism.' But overall I truly believe that we are slowly coming to spiritual maturity.

As a reality check, to make sure that we're not self-deluded, here is what a leading evangelical scholar says about UUA. According to Alan Gomes writing in *Trinity Journal,* his fellow evangelicals "can no longer ignore the Unitarian Universalist Association," because, he says, "the UUA is surprisingly influential, far beyond what its official membership figures suggest." Thus, he concludes, "Unitarian Universalists are often the movers and shakers in society." And what makes us so dangerous is that we proclaim as a saving message "a theology centered on tolerance, interdependence, and compassion." We should get Professor Gomes to write our advertising copy!

A COVENANTAL FAITH

As we face the future, we are also rediscovering the strengths that flow from our heritage. Two pillars of that heritage are congregational polity and the covenantal relationship. They define us not only organizationally but theologically. As Conrad Wright makes clear in his definitive work *Congregational Polity,* "Our polity is important because it defines the way in which we believe human beings should be related to one another for ecclesiastical purposes, and may be a guide or model for human relationships of other kinds."

As for our covenantal tradition, it was reaffirmed when we adopted our Principles and Purposes, which are designed as a covenant, both in form and content. From this tradition, John

Buehrens tells us, flows an obligation to shape the world around us. Indeed, our long-term mission in the world is with others, since doing things with partners "helps to provide the spiritual foundation for a more just, inclusive, and peaceful democracy. . . . Our congregations go back to those that first hit this country more than three hundred years ago, deciding that the basis of congregational life would be democratic, that it would be dedicated to covenant rather than creed."

Covenantal renewal, therefore, he goes on, "captures the best of that heritage and applies it in a new setting—one that is much more multicultural, much more in need of vivid spiritual demonstrations that people of different beliefs, orientations, backgrounds, can not only live together but actually contribute to one another's moral and spiritual growth." The culmination, he concludes, is Unitarian Universalism in a new key: that of spirituality joined to justice making.

Rebecca Parker also stresses the fundamental religious value of covenant. "Can we find a way in which we embrace and celebrate diversity and also cultivate community—something greater than the sum of the parts?" she asks, and suggests that "covenant making may be the key to opening the door to another way of understanding ourselves. The commitments we make to one another, the promises we make to one another as a congregation, as an association, are what creates church community. Covenant requires a human presence, an active presence to one another, and gets us beyond *who am I?* to *who are you?*— and *what can we do together?*"

HOW HIGH THE HOPES AND HURDLES

Those are the promises of our present situation. Whether they will have been fulfilled when someone comes to write the history of our first eighty years depends on how we address certain knife-edge questions. Will we continue to welcome change without losing sight of our heritage and history? Can we pursue diversity without diluting our core beliefs? Find inspiration in the esthetic and the intuitive without either giving up on reason or giving in to sentimentality? Maintain unity of purpose without imposing uniformity of practice or belief? Value individual autonomy without devaluing corporate worship and social action? And finally, will we let ourselves be warmed by a justified pride in our tradition and achievements without forgetting the humility that comes from cool detachment?

These are questions that can be answered only by action, not by words. Of one thing we can be sure, that the need for a faith that stresses the need to ask questions without offering ready-made answers will never become obsolete for, as Carl Jung observed, "The serious problems in life are never really solved."

Theodore Parker said, more than a century ago, "Be ours a religion which, like sunshine, goes everywhere; its temple all space; its shrine the good heart; its creed all truth; its ritual works of love."

If we live up to Parker's vision, ours will still be in 2041 what it was in 1961 and what it remains today: a faith for our time and for the future.

IMPORTANT DATES IN UNITARIAN UNIVERSALIST HISTORY

1568   King John Sigismund (the Unitarian King of Transylvania) proclaims the earliest edict of complete religious toleration.

1648   New England Puritans adopt the Cambridge Platform, establishing the tradition of congregational polity, which still prevails today.

1770   John Murray arrives at Good Luck Point on Barnegat Bay, New Jersey. On September 30, Murray preaches his first sermon in America in the meetinghouse of Thomas Potter.

1785   Liturgy of King's Chapel Boston is revised, omitting references to the Trinity.

1793   Second Universalist Convention in Oxford, Massachusetts, marks founding of precursor of Universalist Church in America.

1796   Joseph Priestly advocates Universalism and Unitarianism in Philadelphia. Founding of the First Unitarian Church of Philadelphia with encouragement of Priestly.

1802   The oldest Pilgrim church in America (founded at Plymouth in 1620) becomes Unitarian.

1805   Hosea Ballou writes *A Treatise on Atonement* (the first book published in America openly rejecting the doctrine of the Trinity).

1811   Harvard Divinity School established.

1819   William Ellery Channing delivers his Baltimore sermon (a landmark statement of Unitarian principles).

1825   The American Unitarian Association (AUA) is organized.

1844   Meadville Theological School established in Meadville, Pennsylvania.

1863   Ordination of Olympia Brown, arguably the first woman to be ordained by any denomination.

1866   Organization of the Universalist General Convention (renamed in 1942 the Universalist Church of America).

1884   The American Unitarian Association becomes an association representative of and directly responsible to its member churches.

1899   First Merger Commission founded.

1900   The International Congress of Free Christians and Other Religious Liberals (today the International Association for Religious Freedom), the oldest international interfaith body, formed.

1901   Beacon Press launched.

1904   Starr King School for the Ministry founded in Berkeley, California, as Pacific Unitarian School of the Ministry.

1931   Second Merger Commission.

1937   Frederick May Eliot elected president of the AUA; Sophia Lyon Fahs appointed children's editor.

1939   Unitarian Service Committee organized.

1944   The Church of the Larger Fellowship organized to serve Unitarians living in areas without Unitarian churches.

1945   The Universalist Service Committee formed.

1953   Liberal Religious Youth, Inc., is formed by the merger of American Unitarian Youth and Universalist Youth Fellowship.

The Council of Liberal Churches (Universalist-Unitarian), Inc., is organized for the federation of the departments of publications, education, and public relations.

1956   Unitarians and Universalists create Joint Commission on Merger to examine feasibility of uniting the two denominations.

1961   The American Unitarian Association and the Universalist Church of America officially consolidate and organize the Unitarian Universalist Association. Dana Greeley elected first president.

1964   James Reeb, Unitarian Universalist minister, murdered in Selma, Alabama, in civil rights protest organized by Martin Luther King, Jr.

1967   Black Unitarian Universalist Caucus organized.

1969   Robert West elected president.

1972   Beacon Press publishes *Pentagon Papers,* and the federal government investigates UUA bank records.

1979   Death of UUA President Paul Carnes; election of President O. Eugene Pickett.

1983   Young Religious Unitarian Universalists (YRUU) succeeds Liberal Religious Youth (LRY).

1985   Election of President William F. Schulz.

$20,000,000 endowment given to the UUA by the North Shore Unitarian Universalist Society of Plandome, New York.

1987 $9,000,000 grant for theological education given to UUA by the North Shore Unitarian Universalist Society of Plandome, New York.

1989   UUA delegation seeking guarantees of religious freedom
        enters Romania two weeks after the revolution. Sister
        (later Partner) church program established between
        UUA and Transylvanian congregations.

1993   Denise Taft Davidoff elected UUA moderator; John A.
        Buehrens elected president.

        International Council of Unitarians and Universalists
        organized.

BIBLIOGRAPHY

BOOKS

Alexander, Scott W., ed. *Salted with Fire: UU Strategies for Sharing Faith and Growing Congregations.* Boston: Skinner House, 1994. Inspiration and practical advice for those seeking to promote the growth of Unitarian Universalism.

Arnason, Wayne B. *Follow the Gleam: A History of the Liberal Religious Youth Movements.* Boston: Skinner House, 1980.

Buehrens, John A., and Forrest Church. *A Chosen Faith.* Boston: Beacon, 1998. An introduction to Unitarian Universalism by two of its most distinguished ministers, with a foreword by Robert Fulghum, best-selling author and UU minister, who has reached vast audiences with highly entertaining essays that convey the message of Unitarian Universalism.

Cassara, Ernest, ed. *Universalism in America: A Documentary History of a Liberal Faith.* Boston: Skinner House, 1997. The story of one of our two founding faiths, told in selected writings from some of the most influential Universalists, together with a brief historical sketch and incisive commentaries by the editor.

Frost, Edward A., ed. *With Purpose and Principle: Essays About the Seven Principles of Unitarian Universalism.* Boston: Skinner House, 1998. A history of the evolution of the Principles, plus essays on their meaning by seven UU ministers. Highly useful for workshops and classes for new Unitarian Universalists.

Goodwin, Joan. *Giving Birth to Ourselves: A History of the Liberal Religious Educators Association, 1949-1999.* San Antonio, TX: Liberal Religious Educators Association, 1999.

Greeley, Dana McLean. *25 Beacon Street and Other Recollections.* Boston: Skinner House, 1971. Required reading for anyone seeking a better understanding of the charismatic first president of the UUA and of the key events during his two terms.

Herz, Walter P., ed. *Redeeming Time: Endowing Your Church with the Power of Covenant.* Boston: Skinner House, 1999. Essays by UU ministers and theologians on the history and current significance of congregational polity.

Jack, Homer A. *Homer's Odyssey: My Quest for Peace and Justice.* Becket, MA: One Peaceful World, 1996. Available from the publisher at PO Box 10, Leland Road, Becket, MA 01223. The fascinating life story of a fascinating man. Includes historic photographs.

———. *WCRP: A History of the World Conference on Religion and Peace.* New York: World Conference on Religion and Peace, 1993.

McKeeman, Gordon. *Out of the Ordinary: Meditations.* Boston: Skinner House, 2000. A book of meditations, reflecting on ways to turn ordinary events into life-enhancing occasions.

Morrison-Reed, Mark. *Black Pioneers in a White Denomination.* 3rd ed. Boston: Skinner House, 1994. The basic volume on its subject.

Owen-Towle, Tom. *O. Eugene Pickett: Borne on a Wintry Wind.* Boston: Skinner House, 1996. The life, personality, and achievements of one of the UUA's most effective presidents.

Robinson, David. "Transcendentalism and Its Time." In *The Cambridge Companion to Ralph Waldo Emerson,* eds. Joel Porte and Saundra Morris. New York: Cambridge University Press, 1999. Rediscovering the genius of liberal religion's greatest writer and philosopher.

———. *Unitarians and the Universalists.* Westport, CT: Greenwood, 1985. The history of both denominations before consolidation. Particularly helpful in tracing the events leading up to consolidation.

Schulz, William F. *Finding Time & Other Delicacies.* Boston: Skinner House, 1992. A collection of essays reflecting on Schulz's beliefs and theological insights, mostly written during his years as UUA president.

Sunley, Robert. *We Started with the Children: From Church School to North Shore Unitarian Society, The Early Years—1941-1955.* UU Congregation at Shelter Rock, NY, 1995.

Unitarian Universalist Association. *Hymns for the Celebration of Life.* Boston: Unitarian Universalist Association, 1964.

———. *Singing the Living Tradition.* Boston: Unitarian Universalist Association, 1993.

Weary, Gerald F. *A Memorial to Caroline E. Veatch, and the History of the Veatch Royalties of the North Shore Unitarian Society.* Plandome, NY: Gerald F. Weary, 1983. Besides telling the story of Caroline Veatch and how she became a benefactress of what is now the UU Congregation at Shelter Rock, New York, it provides details of how Rev. Weary, as its first minister, was instrumental in securing her generous bequest. Available from Gerald Weary, Dyer Neck Road, RFD 1, Newcastle, ME 04553.

Wright, Conrad. *A Stream of Light: A Short History of American Unitarianism.* 2d ed. Boston: Skinner House, 1989. Brief but basic review of Unitarian history leading up to consolidation, by our most distinguished living historian.

———. *Congregational Polity: A Historical Survey of Unitarian and Universalist Practice.* Boston: Skinner House, 1997. Essential background about one of the basic principles of Unitarian Universalism, tracing its roots over four centuries.

ARTICLES, SERMONS, AND LECTURES

Carpenter, Victor. "The Black Empowerment Controversy and the Unitarian Universalist Association, 1967-1970." 1983 Minns Lecture. In *Unitarian Universalism and the Quest for Racial Justice.* Boston: Unitarian Universalist Association, 1993.

Cassara, Ernest. *Hosea Ballou and the Rise of American Religious Liberalism.* Boston: Universalist Historical Society, 1958.

Harrington, Donald S. "Unitarian Universalism: Yesterday, Today, and Tomorrow." Sermon preached at the celebration of the consolidation of the UUA, May 23, 1960.

Harrington, Donald, and Aniko Szatho. "Unitarianism in Transylvania Today." Essay read at Collegium, Craigville, MA, October 1998.

Hotchkiss, Daniel D. "Charles Joy and the Flaming Chalice Symbol." *Journal of Unitarian Universalist History,* vol. 26 (1999).

Hughes, Peter. "The Origins of New England Universalism." *The Journal of Unitarian Universalist History,* vol. 24 (1997).

Murdock, Virgil E. *Minns Lectures: The Institutional History of the American Unitarian Association.* Unitarian Universalist Association, 1975.

Scovel, Carl. "Unitarian Universalism in the Second Millennium." Address at UU Congregation at Shelter Rock, NY, April 1999.

Williams, George Huntston. "The Ministry and the Draft in Historical Perspective." In *The Religious Situation: 1969,* ed. Donald R. Cutler. Boston: Beacon, 1969.

UU PERIODICALS

Connections. A periodical for parents published by the Church of the Larger Fellowship.

Ferment. Published three times a year by the Office of Young Adult/Campus Ministry.

First Days Record: A Journal of Liberal Religious Responses. A collection of contributions by UU ministers, published eight times a year. Subscriptions at $15 per year, c/o UU Fellowship of Newark, 420 Willa Road, Newark, DE 19711.

IARF World. Membership publication of the International Association for Religious Freedom.

InterConnections. A newsletter for congregational leaders. Also available online at www.uua.org/interconnections.

Inward Springs: A Periodical for Liberal Religious Families. Subscriptions $15 per year (4 issues), 48 Old Colony Road, Hartsdale, NY 10530.

Journal of Unitarian Universalist History, The. Formerly *The Proceedings of the Unitarian Universalist Historical Society.*

Partner Church News. Newsletter of the UU Partner Church Council.

Quest. Monthly membership publication of the Church of the Larger Fellowship.

Synapse. Published twice a year for members of YRUU.

UU Voice. A quarterly publication of Unitarian Universalist Advance, P.O. Box 3104, St. Louis, MO 63130.

UU World (and predecessor publications). All member families of UUA member congregations receive it free. Others in United States can subscribe by sending a check for $21 for one year, $40 for two years, or $58 for three years to *UU World,* Lock Box #84571, Boston, MA 02284-5971. Canada and other countries: US $30 a year.

REPORTS AND MISCELLANEOUS

Arnason, Wayne. UUA Commission on Governance report, April 1993.

Buehrens, John. "The Endowment for Theological Education." Report from the Unitarian Universalist Association to the Unitarian Universalist Congregation at Shelter Rock, NY, 1998.

Cole, David H. and Iska. "An Oral History of the Consolidation of the American Unitarian Association and the Universalist Church of America and the Creation of the Unitarian Universalist Association." Unpublished transcripts of interviews. Copies available from David and Iska Cole, 36 Clifford Road, Edgecomb, ME, 04556, iskadave@clinic.net.

Colpitts, Horace. *The Unitarian Universalist District of Metropolitan New York: The First Thirty Years, 1962-1992.* Shoreham, NY: Unitarian Universalist District of Metropolitan New York, 2000.

Free Church in a Changing World, The. Boston: Unitarian Universalist Association, 1963. Reports of six commissions appointed soon after consolidation "to speak to the situation in which the Unitarian Universalist churches now find themselves."

From these Beginnings. Plandome, NY: UU Congregation at Shelter Rock, 1995.

Joint Merger Commission. The Plan to Consolidate the American Unitarian Association and the Universalist Church of America. As approved by the delegates of the AUA and the UCA at Syracuse, NY, on October 31, 1959.

Ladd, Lawrence. Financial Advisor's Report to the 2000 UUA General Assembly, Nashville, TN, June 2000.

Readex, *World* Profile Survey, 1996.

Report of the Coordinating Committee on Consolidation and the

Reports and Recommendations of the Five Interim Committees. Boston: Coordinating Committee on Consolidation, 1961.

Report of the Young Adult Ministries Task Force, UUA, 1987.

Unitarian Universalist Association. Annual Report, 2000.

Unitarian Universalist Association. Annual Treasurer's Report, 2000.

Unitarian Universalist Funding Program. Annual Report, 1999.

UUA Commission on Appraisal. *The Unitarian Universalist Merger, 1961-1975.* Report to the Fourteenth General Assembly of the UUA, 1975.

———. "Empowerment: Our Denomination's Quest for Racial Justice, 1967-1982." In *Unitarian Universalism and the Quest for Racial Justice.* Boston: Unitarian Universalist Association, 1993. 1983 Study of the Unitarian Universalist Association.

———. *Interdependence: Renewing Congregational Polity.* Boston: Unitarian Universalist Association, 1997.

UUA Committee on Compensation, Benefits, and Pensions and the Council on Church Staff Finances. Report on Clergy and Church Staff Compensation, 1997

UUA Continental Youth Adult Committee. "Common Ground 1982." Report to the Unitarian Universalist Association Board of Trustees, 1982.

UUA Youth Assembly Planning Committee. "Common Ground." Report to the Unitarian Universalist Association Board of Trustees, 1981.

UUA Youth Programs Review Committee. Report to the UUA Board of Trustees, 1997.

UU World Staff. Reader Profile Survey, March 1992.

Vendig, Eleanor. *The Caroline Veatch Assistance and Extension Program: An Overview.* Plandome, NY: North Shore Unitarian Society of Plandome, NY (now the UU Congregation at Shelter Rock), 1973.

Wallace and Washburn, Inc. *UU World* Readership Study, Fall 1983.

———. *The World.* Market Research Study, Fall 1987.

Wiseman, Frederick. *UU World* Readership Survey, July 1978.

Young Adult Ministries Task Force. *Working Papers.* Boston: Unitarian Universalist Association, 1987.

YRUU Five-Year Review Committee. *YRUU: A Five-Year Review of Programs for Youth.* Boston: Unitarian Universalist Association, 1989

UUA PAMPHLETS
(AVAILABLE FROM THE UUA BOOKSTORE)

Harris, Mark W. *Unitarian Universalist Origins: Our Historic Faith.*

Hoover, Mel, and James, Jacqui, eds. *Soulful Journeys: The Faith of African American Unitarian Universalists.*

Hotchkiss, Daniel D. *The Flaming Chalice.*

Mendelsohn, Jack. *Meet the Unitarian Universalists.*

Pescan, Barbara J. *Unitarian Universalism: A Religious Home for Bisexual, Gay, Lesbian, and Transgender People.*

Schulman, J. Frank, ed. *Ralph Waldo Emerson Speaks.*

ACKNOWLEDGMENTS

The Introduction notes a few of the people who made special contributions to the development of this book. Many others, through interviews, conversations, personal communications, and the sharing of files, made possible this reconstruction of the story of the Unitarian Universalist Association. Not only did they go out of their way to be helpful but many gave valuable encouragement and guidance. With apologies to anyone who has been inadvertently left out, sincere thanks are due to the following:

Robert Adelman
Rev. Wayne Arnason
Rev. Elinor Artman
Helene Atwan
Rev. Elizabeth Baker (since
    deceased)
Rev. Mark Belletini
Rev. Richard Boeke

Rev. Dwight Brown
Rev. John Buehrens
Freda Carnes
Prof. Ernest Cassara
Denise Davidoff
Rev. Alan Deale
Donna DiSciullo
William Duffy

220 / ACKNOWLEDGMENTS

Judith Frediani
Jerry Gabert
Rev. Max Gaebler
Rev. Charles Gaines
Rev. John Gibbons
Rev. Philip Giles
Mike Gravel
Rev. Harry Green
Natalie Gulbrandsen
Rev. Donald Szantho
  Harrington
Jennifer Harrison
Rev. William Hamilton-
  Holway
Rev. Earl Holt
Jeanette Hopkins
Rev. Raymond Hopkins
Rev. Leon Hopper
Rev. Daniel Hotchkiss
Maude Jenkins, MD
Rev. Walter Royal Jones
Rev. Paul Johnson
Lawrence Ladd
Robert Lavender
Edward Lawrence
Rev. Kenneth Torquil
  MacLean
Rev. Judith Mannheim
Rev. Gordon McKeeman

Rev. Jack Mendelsohn
Rev. Ralph Mero
Duncan Metcalfe
Rev. Diane Miller
Rev. Orloff Miller (to Donna
  DiSciullo)
Kathleen Montgomery
Rev. William Murry
Dr. Winifred Latimer Norman
Rev. Rebecca Parker
Rev. Eugene Pickett
Rev. David Pohl
Norma Poinsett
Prof. David Robinson
Rev. Jane Rzepka
Rev. Harry Scholefield
Rev. William Schulz
Rev. Carl Scovel
Rev. Robert Senghas
Betty Bobo Seiden
Rev. William Sinkford
Katharine Sreedhar
Nathan Staples
Gobin Stair
Wendy Strothman
Robert Sunley
Rev. Malcolm Sutherland
Rev. David Usher
Rev. Robert Nelson West

INDEX

16 Beacon Street, 38
25 Beacon Street, 10-11, 60-61,
    145, 156
About Your Sexuality, 65
Act of Religious Tolerance and
    Freedom of Conscience, 6
Adams, James Luther, 38
Adelman, Robert, 74, 77
Alexander, Scott, 116, 118, 196
American Unitarian
    Association, 4, 8, 13, 19, 26,
    72, 111, 125, 185
American Unitarian Youth, 9,
    142
Andrasi, Gyorgy, 179
Andrews, Barry, 197
Annual Program Fund, 38, 48,
    59, 67, 77, 118-119

Arlington Street Church, 15,
    36-38, 51, 61
Arnason, Wayne, 142, 144-145
Atwan, Helene, 92, 114-115
AUA. *See* American Unitarian
    Association

BAC. *See* Black Affairs Council
Ballou, Hosea, 3-4
Baltimore Sermon, 4
Barr, Margaret, 187
BAWA. *See* Black and White
    Action
Beach, George (Kim), 96
Beacon Press, 62-64, 66, 84, 92,
    111-115
Beacon Song and Service Book,
    104

Belletini, Mark, 100-102, 104
Benton, Eunice, 166
Beyond Categorical Thinking,
    160
Black Affairs Council, 46, 48-55,
    57-59, 143, 161
Black and White Action, 47,
    49-50, 52, 54, 57, 161
Black and White Alternative. *See*
    Black and White Action
Black Caucus. *See* Black Unitar-
    ian Universalist Caucus
Black Concerns Working Group,
    161
Black Unitarian Universalist
    Caucus, 44, 46-49,
    51-52, 55
Blue Book. *See* Plan to Consoli-
    date
Boeke, Richard, 37, 90
Brown, Dwight, 53
Buehrens, John, ix-xi, 71, 116-
    117, 119, 167, 169, 173-174,
    182-183, 187, 193, 195, 200,
    203-205
BUUC. *See* Black Unitarian
    Universalist Caucus

C*UUYAN. *See* Continental UU
    Young Adults Network
Campaign for Unitarian Uni-
    versalism, 79, 119
Čapek, Norbert, 90
Carnes, Paul, 83-84, 156, 168
Caroline Veatch Assistance and
    Extension Program, 60, 71,
    75-76, 78, 120, 133, 140,
    149, 159, 178
Caron, Sandra, 113, 157, 192-193
Carpenter, Victor, 46
Cassara, Ernest, 10, 16, 191, 198
Cavenaugh, Rob, 182
chalice. *See* flaming chalice

Channing Murray Foundation,
    9, 148
Channing, William Ellery, 3-5
Christian Leader. See *Universal-
    ist Leader*
Christian Register. See *Unitar-
    ian Register*
Church of the Larger
    Fellowship, 109-111, 121
Clarke, James Freeman, 11
CLC. *See* Council of Liberal
    Churches
CLF. *See* Church of the Larger
    Fellowship
Cole, Alfred S., 9
College Centers Office, 148
Commission of Appraisal, 13, 18
    See also Commission on
    Appraisal
Commission on Appraisal, 47,
    50
    See also Commission of
    Appraisal
Commission on Worship, 84
Committee to Study Theologi-
    cal Education, 125
Common Ground, 145
Common Vision, 159
Congress for Racial Equality, 36
Connections, 110
Continental Conference on
    Women and Religion, 94
Continental UU Young Adults
    Network, 149-150
Coordinating Committee on
    Consolidation, 24-25
CORE. *See* Congress for Racial
    Equality
Corrado, John, 104
Council of Liberal Churches, 9,
    14, 21
Council on Ministerial Educa-
    tion, 141

Crane Theological School, 124
Creating a Jubilee World, 165
CUC. *See* Council of Liberal
  Churches
Cummins, John, 96

David, Francis, 6
Davidoff, Denise, ix, 95-96, 157,
  165, 187, 193, 203
De Benneville, George, 6
Deale, Alan, 39, 59
Department of Congregational,
  District, and Extension
  Services, 121
Department of Extension, 118
Department of Ministerial and
  Congregational Services,
  68, 84
Department of Ministry,
  126-127
Department of Religious Edu-
  cation, 138
Department of Service, 25
Department of Social Responsi-
  bility, 36, 66, 84, 167
Deutsch, Hans, 87-89
Dias, Robette, 166
Dimock, Marshall E., 32-33, 193
DiSciullo, Donna, 150-151
Donovan, William A., 23
Duffy, William, 64

Electronic Communications
  Committee, 108
Eliot, Frederick May, 9, 13, 16,
  21, 86
Ellsberg, Daniel, 62
Emergency Conference on
  Unitarian Universalist
  Response to the Black
  Rebellion, 45, 47

Fahs, Sophia, 155

Faith in Action: A UUA Depart-
  ment for Diversity and Jus-
  tice, 169
Federal Bureau of Investigation,
  63-64
Fellowship Committee. *See*
  Ministerial Fellowship
  Committee
Ferber, Michael, 37
Ferment, 151
Fisher, Carleton, 48
Fisher, Joseph, 33, 51, 68-69,
  193
Fisher, Margaret, 51
flaming chalice, 88-90
flower communion, 90
Foote, Arthur, 100-101, 104
Frediani, Judith, 92, 139-140
Free Church of America, 9
Friends of the UUA, 79, 120
Frost, Edward A., 92, 94, 97
Full Support of BAC, 48-50, 52
FULLBAC. *See* Full Support of
  BAC
Fund for Racial Justice, 49

Gaebler, Max, 33, 50, 53, 171,
  182
Gaines, Charles, 191
Gannett, Ezra, 44, 149
Gellerd, Judit, 178-179
Gibbons, John, 180-181
Giles, Philip, 16, 21, 24, 27,
  30-32, 38, 40
Gold, Bill, 143
Gomes, Alan, 204
Goodwin, Joan, 141
Gravel, Mike, 62-64
Greeley, Dana McLean, 14-16,
  21, 25, 27, 29-40, 43-44, 48,
  50-51, 59-60, 77, 86-87,
  117, 120, 125, 167, 171, 177,
  182, 193, 195

Guild, Polly and Ted, 174
Gulbrandsen, Natalie, 93-95, 156-157, 173, 178-179, 193, 198

Hampton, Henry, 46
Handing on the Future, 79, 119
Harrington, Donald Szantho, 19-20, 23, 52, 276-178
Harrison, Jennifer, 146-148
Harvard Divinity School, 10, 58, 124, 132
Harvie, Kim Crawford, 159
Henry, Heyward, 44-45, 49
Herndon, David, 89
Hoehler, Harry, 97
Holdeen Asia Fund, 187
Holdeen India Program, 184-186
Holdeen, Jonathan, 185
Holmes, John Haynes, 46
Holmes, Olivia, 182
Hoover, Melvin, 56, 161, 165
Hopkins, Jeanette, 54-55, 112-113,
Hopkins, Raymond C., 16, 20-22, 24-25, 30-31, 35, 38-40
Hopper, Leon, 179-180, 190
Hotchkiss, Dan, 88, 90
Human Sexuality, 65
Hymnbook Commission. See Hymnbook Resources Commission
Hymnbook Resources Commission, 84, 102-104
Hymns for the Celebration of Life, 100-101, 104

IARF. See International Association for Religious Freedom
ICUU. See International Council of Unitarians and Universalists

InterConnections, 107
International Association for Liberal Christianity and Religious Freedom, 172
See also International Association for Religious Freedom
International Association for Religious Freedom, 94, 121, 171-173, 175, 177
See also International Association for Liberal Christianity and Religious Freedom
International Council of Unitarian and Other Liberal Religious Thinkers and Workers. See International Association for Religious Freedom
International Council of Unitarians and Universalists, 175-176
Interweave, 159

Jack, Homer, 36, 43, 46-48, 53-54, 168, 171, 182
Jenkins, Maude, 46
Johnson, Paul, 130, 199
Joint Merger Commission, 9, 16, 19, 21-22, 27
Jones, Walter Royal, 96-99, 200
Journey Toward Wholeness, 162-165, 167, 169
Journey Toward Wholeness Transformation Committee, 163
Joy, Charles, 87-88

Kapp, Max, 33
King, Martin Luther, 42-45
Kovacs, Sandor, 180
Kring, Walter Donald, 21
Kuebler, Ernest, 177

Ladd, Lawrence, 53, 117-119, 143
Lavender, Robert, 115
Lawrence, Edward, 77
Liberal Religious Educators Association, 141
Liberal Religious Youth, 9, 49, 67, 142-145
Liuzzo, Viola Gregg, 43
LREDA. *See* Liberal Religious Educators Association
LRY. *See* Liberal Religious Youth

MacLean, Kenneth, 174, 183, 186-187
Massachusetts Universalist Convention, 38
McBroom, Marcia, 52
McCree, Wade, 48
McDade, Carolyn, 159
McDougald, Cornelius, 46-47
McGinness, Mason, 27
McGorrill, Milton, 27
McKeeman, Gordon, xiv, 69, 84-85, 132, 134, 190, 194
Meadville/Lombard, 58, 124-125, 129-130, 132-133, 141, 181
Mendelsohn, Jack, 36-37, 51, 61, 64, 84, 190, 198
Merger Commission. *See* Joint Merger Commission
Mero, Ralph, 133-134
Meyers, Suzanne P., 197
MFC. *See* Ministerial Fellowship Committee
Millennium World Peace Summit of Religious and Spiritual Leaders, 183
Miller, Diane, 127, 130, 156-157
Miller, Joel, 116
Miller, Orloff, 43, 149
Ministerial Education Office, 126

Ministerial Fellowship Committee, 121, 126-128, 132
Ministerial Sisterhood of Unitarian Universalists, 130, 157
Modified Residency Program, 133
MSUU. *See* Ministerial Sisterhood of Unitarian Universalists
Montgomery, Kay, 160-162, 174, 190, 193
Morgan, John, 118
Morrison-Reed, Mark, 45, 161
Muir, Frederic, 188
Murdock, Virgil, 4
Murray Grove Unitarian Universalist conference center, 5
Murray, John, 5-6
Murry, William, 129, 131, 135

National Federation of Religious Liberals, 9
National Inter-Religious Conference on Peace, 35
Navias, Eugene, 159
New Congregation Ministry Program, 117
New England Universalist Publishing House, 111
Nickerson, James, 74
Niwano, Nikkyo, 182
Norman, Winifred Latimer, 47
North Shore Unitarian Society, 49, 71-75, 78-79
See also Unitarian Universalist Congregation at Shelter Rock

Office of Bisexual, Gay, Lesbian, and Transgender Concerns, 157
See also Office of Gay Affairs

Office of Church Staff Finances, 133
Office of Electronic Communications, 107
Office of Gay Affairs, 66, 157
    See also Office of Bisexual, Gay, Lesbian, and Transgender Concerns
Office of International Relations, 182
Office of Social Responsibility, 168
Office of Young Adult/Campus Ministry, 150
Office on Aging, 66
Olsen, Clark, 43, 199
Opus, 149
Osborne, David, 132
Our Whole Lives, 66, 139, 158
Overseas and Interfaith Relations Department, 171
Owen-Towle, Carolyn S., 157
Owen-Towle, Tom, 68, 94, 121, 168

P&P. *See* Principles and Purposes
Parker, Rebecca, xiii, 130-131, 134-135, 197, 205
Parker, Theodore, 206
Parliament of the World's Religions, 183
Partner Church Council, 180, 182
Pentagon Papers, 62-64, 112
Pescan, Barbara, 158
Pickett, O. Eugene, 67-68, 79, 84-85, 91, 94, 110, 119-120, 126, 149, 159, 161, 168, 172, 193, 198
Plan for Merger, 17
Plan to Consolidate, 17
Plebiscite Committee, 22

Pohl, David, 84, 128, 131-132, 158, 190
Poinsett, Norma, 55
Potter, Thomas, 5
President's Council, 195
Priestly, Joseph, 6
Principles and Purposes, 18, 28, 91-100, 114, 200, 204

Quest, 109-110
Quimada-Sienes, Rebecca, 188

Rapid Start, 121
RE. *See* Department of Religious Education
Reeb, James, 42-44
Register-Leader, 106
Rex, John, 187
Rice, William, 16, 18, 30
Robinson, David M., xiv, 9, 14
Rzepka, Jane, 109-110, 201

Schade, Tom, 166-167
Scholefield, Harry, 59
Schulz, William, 30-31, 35, 61, 79, 84, 106, 119, 161-162, 168, 174, 178, 192-193, 198
Schweitzer, Albert, 180
Scovel, Carl, 40, 59, 96, 105, 125-126
Seiden, Betty Bobo, 48, 52, 56
Selma, 42-44
Senghas, Robert, 66, 160
Service of the Living Tradition, 123
Settlement Office, 127
Sharing in Growth, 67, 119
Sigismund, King John, 5
Singh, Hajom Kissor, 187
Singing the Living Tradition, 100-104
Sinkford, William, 120-121, 143-144, 195, 200

Skinner House Books, 111
Skinner, Clarence, 111
Social Witness Commission, 169
Sreedhar, Katharine, 185-186
St. Lawrence, 124
Stair, Gobin, 62-65
Staples, Nathan, 147
Starr King School for the Min-
    istry, 58, 84-85, 124-125,
    130-132, 181
Starr King, Thomas, 8
Stites, Thomas, 106
Straub, Arvid, 197
Strong, Douglas Morgan, 158
Strothman, Wendy, 92, 113-114
Student Religious Liberals, 149
Sunley, Robert, 22, 72
Synapse, 110, 146

Taylor Report, 125
Taylor, Harold, 125
Thandeka, 166
Ticknor, George, 44
Transylvania, 5-6, 176-181
Treadwell, Anne, 92
Trust for Theological Educa-
    tion, 132-133

UCA. See Universalist Church
    of America
Unitarian Laymen's League, 86
Unitarian Regions, 26
Unitarian Register, 25, 106
Unitarian Service Committee,
    25, 27, 87, 176
Unitarian Union of North East
    India, 187
Unitarian Universalist Commis-
    sion on Religion and Race,
    45-47
Unitarian Universalist Congre-
    gation at Shelter Rock, 60,
    71, 78-79, 132

See also North Shore Unitar-
    ian Society
Unitarian Universalist Funding
    Program, 78
Unitarian Universalist Minis-
    ters' Association, 179
Unitarian Universalist Service
    Committee, 38, 66, 84, 90
Unitarian Universalist United
    Nations Office, 184
Unitarian Universalist Women's
    Federation, 93, 95-96,
    156-157
Unitarian Universalist World.
    See *UU World*
Unitarian Universalists for Les-
    bian and Gay Concerns, 159
United Liberal Church of Amer-
    ica, 14, 17
Universalist Church of America,
    9, 11, 16
Universalist General Conven-
    tion, 8, 11
Universalist Leader, 25, 106
Universalist Service Commit-
    tee, 25, 32
Universalist State Conventions,
    11, 25
Universalist Youth Fellowship, 9
Usher, David, 173-175
uu&me, 110
UUA Goals Committee, 117
UUA Now, 106
UUA website, 107-108, 111
UUMA. *See* Unitarian Univer-
    salist Ministers' Associa-
    tion
UUSC. *See* Unitarian Universal-
    ist Service Committee
UUWF. *See* Unitarian Universal-
    ist Women's Federation
UU World, 66-67, 97, 106-107,
    112, 142, 158-159, 191, 199

Veatch Board of Governors, 76, 78
Veatch, Caroline, 72-75
Veatch Committee. *See* Veatch Board of Governors
Veatch program. *See* Caroline Veatch Assistance and Extension Program.
Vendig, Eleanor, 76-77
Visions for Growth, 79, 119

Wagner, Julia, 72
WCRP. *See* World Conference on Religion and Peace
Weary, Gerald F., 72-74
Weaving the Fabric of Diversity, 166
Welcoming Congregation Program, 159, 166, 169
West, Robert N., 18, 53, 57-62, 64-69, 76, 105, 119, 126, 157, 172, 193
Western Unitarian Conference, 39
Williams, Betsy Hill, 110
Williams, George H., 37
Winchester Confession, 8
Women and Religion resolution, 93-95
Women in Religion Committee, 156
Women's Federation. *See* Unitarian Universalist Women's Federation
World. See *UU World*
World Conference on Religion and Peace, 182-183
Wright, Conrad, 8, 204

Young Adult Caucus, 150
Young Adult Ministries Task Force, 149

Young Religious Unitarian Universalists, 145-150
YRUU. *See* Young Religious Unitarian Universalists